THE SOCIAL THEORIES OF
L. T. HOBHOUSE

The Social Theories of
L. T. Hobhouse

By HUGH CARTER, Ph.D.

KENNIKAT PRESS, INC./PORT WASHINGTON, N. Y.

THE SOCIAL THEORIES OF L. T. HOBHOUSE

Copyright 1927 by The University of North Carolina Press
Reissued in 1968 by Kennikat Press
Library of Congress Catalog Card No: 67-27609
Manufactured in the United States of America

PREFACE

Writing a critical summary of a living scholar's work is a decidedly delicate operation. Attempting to indicate the forces that have molded his work, particularly when that work has been carried on in a country known to the reviewer only through a visit of a few months duration, makes the task hazardous. It has been more customary to select for study and review the writings of someone safely dead. There is an obvious advantage in such procedure since the writer's completed works may be viewed in historic perspective. Such an operation, however, when dealing with social theory, loses something in that a changed world and the advance of knowledge may require a different emphasis. Also, from the standpoint of sportsmanship, the contemporary review has all the advantage. No one need turn in one's grave; all the turning can take place in a less restricted area.

With the short-comings of this little volume none can be more conversant than its writer; he can only plead in mitigation that he has spent long hours with the works of this great English philosopher and sociologist and has made the attempt to set forth the contributions of Hobhouse to social science within the limits of a few pages.

The writer appreciates deeply the help he has received from many friends, not here mentioned, who have given information or have assisted in one way or another in completing the study. Especially does he wish to thank the scholars in England who have assisted. He has to thank Mr. L. T. Hobhouse for going over the bibliography of his own writings and making certain corrections and other suggestions. Mr. Graham Wallas, Miss Winifred Cramp, Mr. Stephen Hobhouse, and the Assistant Warden of Toynbee House have all placed the writer under obligation to them by the assistance freely given him.

The primary debt of the writer, however, is to Mr. Alvan A. Tenney of Columbia University who originally suggested the study and who has assisted in every possible way in carrying it through. To Mr. Franklin H. Giddings he is indebted for many suggestions and much encouragement in working on the project. To Mr. Keith Carter his thanks are due for many useful suggestions and for a careful reading of the galley proofs. Mr. Stuart Rice read a section of the manuscript and made certain suggestions.

H. C.

UNIVERSITY OF PENNSYLVANIA,
   PHILADELPHIA,
      June 1927.

CONTENTS

I. INTRODUCTION

How easy it is to damn a man with a phrase. Some years ago the writer was introduced to Leonard T. Hobhouse by a lecturer stating: "The leading English sociologist, Hobhouse, is primarily a philosopher." Primarily a philosopher! The lecturer went on to say many things about this man, doubtless very complimentary, but the student did not hear. He was not listening. Following the usual taboo of American social science upon philosophy as a thing accursed he dismissed this scholar from his mind. Perhaps this experience is rather typical; perhaps it helps to explain the neglect of Hobhouse's writings in America during the past two decades. For this scholar is obviously a philosopher turned social scientist and carrying with him the limitations of such a transition.

Yet why should he turn from problems of metaphysics and logic to those of the hum-drum world? The explanation lies partly in the man, partly in the times in which he lived. The last three decades of the nineteenth century were turbulent years. Everyone had been upset by the theory of evolution put abroad shortly before and now Spencer was adding new turmoil by amplifying his extension of that theory to cover every phase of development,—inorganic, organic, and "superorganic." This last includes man's most cherished possessions of morality, religion, forms of family, etc. Spencer also held to a laissez-faire philosophy which led him to point out many of the stupidities and follies resulting from state interference with processes going on in society. Now to the young Hobhouse this Spencerian view amounted to the proposition that progress was possible only through allowing natural selection and the survival of the fit to operate in unchecked vigor and ruthlessness. To him this was unthinkable, for progress took place through coöperation and a consequent checking of ruthless struggle. It was becoming popular in England to justify the worst aspects of industrial society with its pauperism and misery by parroting certain phrases,—"natural selection," "survival of the fit"—lifted from the literature of evolution. That this was a complete misinterpretation of Spencer and other authorities was of slight significance to those who simply desired apparent scientific excuses for a situation that from a humane point of view had no justification.

Under the circumstances what was a philosopher to do? So disturbing had the world of science become, with its new discoveries and endless controversies, that one was tempted to give up all consideration of it. How soothing after the turmoil of scientific discussion to retire to an ivory tower and there survey life and eternity, leaving entirely out of mind the doings of certain vulgar fellows in laboratories. And there were philosophers of that period, as there are of every period, who did just that. Yet such a flight from reality was unattractive to Hobhouse. He turned rather to a detailed consideration of the process of evolution itself.

This study of evolution led him eventually to think of progress as an application of intelligence to the complex of changes going on in the world about him, and —by happy coincidence—this did not involve reversing the trend of events in human history but rather a speeding up of a process that had been going on for centuries. This was all very well provided there was the intelligence to be applied. What of the proposition put forth by certain unpleasant people that man is only a reacting mechanism; that cause and effect, stimulus and response, chase each other so closely through the life of man from birth to death that at no point can

Will or Individual Choice break in to interrupt the sequence? To this question Hobhouse devoted years of attention, considering it philosophically, psychologically, and historically. A brief resumé of his position with certain criticisms is given elsewhere; here it is enough to state that for him man indubitably has mind and the freedom of will to apply it if only he can be persuaded to do so.

Presuming, then, man's application of intelligence to his own betterment, Hobhouse holds that progress will take place in several directions. The individual will look to the giving of sane outlets to all the basic needs of his personality. Yet these "root interests" can only be satisfied in a changed world and it will be necessary to go about the task of so modifying the organization of society that the socially useful work will always carry with it the possibility of the personality of the worker expanding. Moreover true progress comes through a realization that individual well-being and societal well-being are two aspects of the same thing.

The individual wishes a consistent and well-integrated personality—he wishes "harmony." Yet real harmony for the individual is impossible without harmony in his group, and eventually this group must include all humanity. Now for Hobhouse history gives us a picture of a world moving in the direction of greater and greater harmony. This comes first within the small group, which gradually increases in size. Philosophically this leads to a conception of universal harmony and of Reality animated by a great Spirit or Effort working toward Universal Harmony. This conception, however, lies outside the field of social theory as here considered. It is recorded simply to aid in understanding the man whose works are to be examined.

Naturally enough Hobhouse is a rationalist in philosophy.

In the present study only so much of his metaphysical theory and of his discussion of the logical basis and validity of human knowledge is included as seems necessary to make his "social theory" clear. Social theory as here used includes the origin and functioning of human society, the problems of adjustment in the individual and society, and certain closely related matters. There is a sense in which most phases of social theory can be reduced, logically, to a matter of philosophic theory. If one is interested in social progress one naturally inquires, progress toward *what,* and this leads to a consideration of those things that are ultimately good and desirable for mankind. Yet speculation about the ultimate good has proved barren. The scientific procedure seems to lie in setting up proximate ends based on criteria objective and subject to test. These ends and the means of attaining them are subject to revision with advancing knowledge. Consequently, while the philosophic theory of Hobhouse may be of great value in philosophy it has no place in social theory.

In his consideration of mind and mechanism a prolonged study of the intellectual factor in evolution is carried through. Here and in the bulk of his other writings Hobhouse leans heavily on psychological theory. One naturally asks—What psychological theory? A question easier to ask than adequately to answer. One may say at once that he is a cautious and rather discriminating introspectionist. He is much given to detailed (sometimes illuminating) scrutiny and dissection of psychological problems. Unfortunately, much of this work is marred by continued use of McDougall's instinct categories. Hobhouse has not by any means relied entirely upon introspection in sketching mental evolution but has used extensively biological history and experimental results of others as well as his own. Now his psychological experiments, carried through with care upon a variety of animals, have their place in a history of experimental psychology; they have only limited value otherwise, as they were performed without adequate controls.

After the study of mental evolution detailed consideration is given to social evolution. This work falls naturally into two parts; primitive societies, and those societies having written records. Regarding primitive society Hobhouse has used the comparative method with great care. To this he has added a statistical treatment of his own devising and this the cautious student cannot accept at its face value. His sketch of social evolution from the beginning of written records is both scholarly and highly thought provoking. It is a real contribution to social thinking.

The attention to social evolution is a part of Hobhouse's interest in politics and in proposals for economic and social reform. When very young he leaned toward socialism but shifted to liberalism. During a long life he has set forth with vigor and clarity his views upon the issues of the day. He has done this with rare detachment, probably a natural judicial temperament being augmented by prolonged study of the history of society. Be that as it may, it remains true that one of his important contributions has been a scrutiny of fundamental social problems and the setting down of rational lines of solution for them.

In social ethics Hobhouse has the advantage of being able to hold the evolutionary process vividly before him while the vexatious present problem is turned over in his mind. Only during the periods of the Boer War and the World War, when everything he held dear seemed crashing to ruin, did he lose his detached viewpoint. The writings of those periods are vigorous if

not judicial. Yet even during the World War, his thinking when compared with most other scholars close to
the war is both clear and detached.

When Hobhouse turned from philosophy to sociology
it is not to be assumed that he turned all the way.
There is more than a thread of consistency running
through his life; in fact one looks in vain for any important strand of activity that has been snapped off.
In simple truth, Hobhouse has given a broad philosophic setting and justification for the English human-
istic trend that has found its most congenial political
home in the "Left Wing" of the Liberal Party.

One naturally inquires as to the personal life of Hobhouse, of his family, education, and the factors influencing him more intimately than the broad happen-
ings of politics and industry.

Leonard Hobhouse was the son of a Cornish archdeacon of the Church of England, Venerable Hobhouse,
Archdeacon of Trelawny. His family belonged to the
small landed aristocracy; his mother was Caroline,
daughter of Sir William Trelawny. The mother came
from an artistic, adventurous family with a bit of Celtic
strain in it. Against the strict religious views of his
father the boy reacted strongly as he approached maturity. The father was a strict High Churchman. However, the son's writings are imbued with a belief in
some supernatural Effort, underlying reality, a force
attempting to shape it to universal harmony. In his
Development and Purpose he attempts an elaborate
philosophical justification of these views, and it is easy
to trace a thread of the early religious training in all
this.

Both at Oxford and in his earlier preparation, Leo-
nard Hobhouse gave evidence of his intellectual gifts.
At Marlborough College he belonged to the "Upper
Sixth" of the school, a curiously mature group for a

preparatory school. He worked vigorously on Greek and Latin literature and history and in due time went up to Oxford as a scholar in one of the small, well endowed colleges. Here there was much more of Greek and Latin to be imbibed and a great lot of philosophy, but there was also a quickening of interest in history and the rising social movement. This was in the days when Hegel's influence was waning.

When twenty-three years old, Hobhouse became a Fellow in Merton College; at twenty-six was Assistant Tutor and at thirty a Fellow in the large and important Christ Church College. Meanwhile his interest in social matters led him to take part in an attempt to organize the agricultural workers about Oxford. These laborers were still in a wretchedly depressed condition, having been left behind by the none too prosperous urban workers. However, in the traditional Tory conservatism of Oxford, his efforts were none too welcome.

At this time two forces were attracting Hobhouse in opposite directions. On the one hand he was fairly well placed in Oxford and a quiet home life devoted to academic pursuits appealed strongly to him. On the other hand, Oxford, the home of lost causes, had little interest in the social movement that gripped him, and scant respect for it. He found his world cramping. He longed to take part in the broader fields of politics and social reform. The two poles of his thinking are well illustrated in two of his books of this period: *The Labour Movement* ('93) and *The Theory of Knowledge* ('96). The latter is a large and pretentious volume going over the logical and philosophical grounds of human knowledge. It is unbelievably dull. The *Labour Movement* is a very small book. It is entirely unpretentious, yet its style is spritely and at times sparkling. Strongly held convictions are evident and deep indignation at the evils of the almost unchecked competitive society of England in the nineties.

This conflict of desires in the young Hobhouse was happily resolved. C. P. Scott, editor of the Manchester *Guardian* and an old member of his college, asked Hobhouse to come and write for that notable liberal paper. Rumor has it that on his first visit to the *Guardian* office he wrote an excellent "leader" though he had had no previous experience as a journalist. For five turbulent years he was one of the important editorial writers for that paper.

Hobhouse went to Manchester in '97. He was then thirty-three years old. Events in South Africa began moving ominously and two years later the Boer War broke. Both through the editorial pages of the *Guardian* and as a leader of opinion in the Manchester area, he did his utmost to bring the war to an end and to secure a just peace for the Boers.

During the Boer War, Emily Hobhouse, the energetic older sister of Leonard Hobhouse, took a leading part in the protests against the continuance of the war. Certain friends of Hobhouse have indicated that in those early years he was much influenced in social movements by his sister and so her activities are of more than casual interest to anyone wishing to understand her brother's development. Emily Hobhouse made a first hand study of conditions in the prison camps in South Africa and returning to England held meetings of protest against British policy and raised relief funds. Though hampered by the government her activities continued and after the war she established industrial schools for the Boers in South Africa. With these facts in mind one reads *Democracy and Reaction* with a new understanding of its vigorous protest against British imperialism and the Boer War.

Characteristically enough, in the midst of his vigorous journalistic activity Hobhouse did not lose touch with things academic. He was Professor of Sociology in Owens College, now the University of Manchester, during his stay in Manchester. Within the same period he completed his *Mind in Evolution,* published in 1901.

In 1900 he became Secretary of the Free Trade Union, giving this up in 1905 to become editor of the short-lived *Tribune* in London. This paper set forth with vigor the views of left-wing Liberalism and in general supported Mr. Lloyd George (then in his early radical phase) in the movement to redress social ills through legislative means. Throughout his career Hobhouse has worked consistently for such things as Old Age Pensions, Trade Boards, Land Reform, and for a reduction of expenditures on armaments. In 1907, the year after publication of his *Morals in Evolution,* he went to the University of London, as Professor of Sociology in its School of Economics. Despite poor health and the burdens of academic work, Hobhouse has carried forward a large amount of public work. He has been chairman of seven or eight Trade Boards.

The normality of Hobhouse's early career is striking. He went to the right school, studied the right subjects, got the scholarship and fellowship at Oxford that was expected. Yet a sensitive mind, reacting to important changes in the world he lived in, gave results that must have surprised many.

II. PREHUMAN ADAPTATION IN THE EVOLUTIONARY PROCESS

"Development" is perhaps the most meaningful word in the Hobhouse vocabulary. Years of patient scholarship have been devoted to a study of development in its many phases. Whether we speak of the evolution of plant or animal or social institution we are considering a subject this writer has given long attention. A cautious introspectionist in psychology, a deeply convinced rationalist in philosophy, Hobhouse has turned an Oxford trained mind, with the values and limitations of prolonged study of the classics, upon the problem of the prehuman stage of adaptation to the requirements of life. We are here concerned with sketching the views of Hobhouse regarding the increasing importance of mind in the evolutionary process.

One naturally inquires why the extraordinary interest of this writer in development? Again one recalls the terrific intellectual struggle of the last quarter of the nineteenth century—precipitated by Darwin's *Origin of Species* and abetted by Spencer's extension of the evolutionary principle to include every phase of existence. In Spencer there is more than a suggestion of a mechanistic world and from mechanism Hobhouse turned away with complete distaste. Yet the young philosopher, who was beginning to be interested also in science, saw that if the world is to be built around *mind* then in the evolutionary process *mind* must inevitably play an increasing role. Did it? The young philosopher did not know but he went about finding out with a right good will.

For Hobhouse the easy assumption that "progress" and "evolution" are synonymous terms is not to be lightly accepted if the concept of "progress" has any rational meaning. What evolution does is to accentuate types; it does not necessarily improve; it cuts deep and spaces out the types. Even when higher forms develop, lower ones indefinitely persist and oftentimes a lower form overcomes one above it. For Hobhouse, then, it is the growth of mind that is most important in the evolutionary process. Hence he is concerned with what he calls "Orthogenic" or "Aristogenic" evolution, *i.e.,* the growth of the mind. The functioning of mind is considered from the point of view of a man long immersed in philosophic thought who watches it at work adjusting the organism to its environment.

And after all the study what conclusion did the scholar reach? That mind is by all odds the most important thing in the evolutionary process; that it becomes increasingly significant at each step forward of the process, and that so far as man is concerned a mechanistic interpretation of his behavior has the weight of evidence lying heavily against it.

Of course this is leaving to one side the question whether mind and mechanism are essentially different. Needless to state this is a very fundamental question for Hobhouse. In brief, he holds that as far as concerns higher living organisms both mind and mechanism are clearly present; mechanism is seen in the marvelous and entirely unconscious manner in which the organism adapts itself to the changes of geographical environment, and mind in the way past experience is brought to bear upon solving a strange problem.

And what are the functions of mind? They are concerned with bringing together things that have a bearing upon one another. "Where there is mind there are order and system, correlation and proportion, a harmonizing of forces, and an interconnection of parts."[1] Unorganized action is unintelligent action. The more highly developed the mind the more diverse the things that can be brought together for use in solving a problem. A trained bridge-builder, called upon to span the Mississippi, would bring to his aid all the lore of his predecessors on bridge building. Correlation is then the yardstick; by it we measure the amount of mind present in any case considered.

All of which is like giving the conclusion of a story before the characters have been introduced. And yet, like the conclusion of many a story, it is not so simple as to be compressed into a few phrases. We turn to a consideration of adaptations in the evolutionary process before the level of *homo sapiens* has been reached.

Various aspects of the adjustment of living things to their environment might be considered—the webbed feet of the duck or the protective coloring of innumerable forms of life. Such things are drastically omitted by Hobhouse. The stages in the development of mind alone interest us. Beginning with elemental forms of response we pass to the more complex.

First consideration may be given to the reflex—one of the simpler forms of response. Hobhouse uses the term reflex to cover cases in which "a simple sensory stimulus calls forth a uniform reaction on the part of the organism."[2] However there is some confusion in his use of the term for it includes involuntary batting of the eyelids upon approach of an object and modifiable conduct like "weeping, screaming, and groaning."[3] One is left a bit bewildered at times in his discussion of the reflex; are we dealing with simple unmodifiable conduct, or a conditioned reflex, or a habit? When concerned with the modification of some simple

[1] *Mind in Evolution,* p. 6.
[2] *Ibid.,* p. 41.
[3] *Ibid.,* p. 42.

"inherited" reflex Hobhouse does not use the familiar
phrase "conditioned reflex." For a long time it was
difficult to make even a respectable conjecture in explanation of this omission. That he was unfamiliar with
the voluminous literature from Pavlov to Watson on
the conditioned reflex was unlikely. However, if one
follows clear through the Hobhousian position regarding the supreme importance of Mind in the evolutionary process, it is not difficult to see why he would not
be enthusiastic over a phrase so closely identified with
the mechanistic interpretation of behavior.

At the lowest level, Hobhouse maintains, reflex is a
result of the excitability of protoplasm. Natural selection operating over a long period of time stamps in a
particular pattern of behavior. Among the lower organisms, where reflex obviously plays such an important
role, each reflex tends on the whole to preserve the life
of the species. As both organism and environment become more complex the rigidly invariable response of
the reflex becomes progressively less successful in
meeting the survival problem. For that matter rigid and
invariable response is never a notable success. Even
among lower insects the species only manage to survive through unusual diligence in producing young—
most of whom die before reaching maturity. As a result, very far down in the scale another form of adjustment is to be observed—instinct.

The word "instinct" raises at once an exceedingly
controversial subject. It may clarify the discussion to
state that Hobhouse follows McDougall rather closely
in his views on instinct and its significance in the
life of an organism. For him instinct cannot be used
to explain everything in animal life, and its territory
is not apart but strictly continuous with other powers
of the organism. While the "more plastic instincts" bear
a close relation to purposive conduct the two are never

to be confused for they are different both in origin and content. Instinct comes before experience and intelligence after it. Instinctive behavior (as of the emperor moth skillfully weaving its cocoon) is not learned from parents and is a skill without parallel in other activities of the particular organism. What is the basis of instinct? Beyond doubt it lies in the hereditary structure. Are we then to think of it as a chain of reflexes? No, answers Hobhouse, it is more than that; the hen has a "maternal instinct," giving set and direction to all her activities. Also, reflex action is unconscious, and instinctive action conscious. In the same way we are not to think of instincts as entirely mechanical since many of them are imperfect at birth and a differing environment brings variation in the operation of the instinct. Within narrow limits intelligence may modify instinct, so we find in the same animal contrasts of stupidity and intelligence. In one situation the animal modifies instinct and succeeds in solving a problem, in another he entirely fails.

How does it come about in the process of evolution that intelligence replaces instinct? Through a gradual process. Intelligence first perceives the immediate next step toward which instinct is driving and modifies conduct the more quickly to reach that step; later the ultimate goal toward which instinct drives is also perceived and then intelligence may vary the whole process, having in mind only the end-result. Instinct, then, "is an enduring interest determined by heredity and directing action to results of importance to the organism without clear prevision of those results. Pure instinct is an interest so controlling internally determined activities, reflexes, and sensori-motor actions. A single sensori-motor act would fall within the limits of the definition only if the interest prompting it were hereditary and enduring. In point of fact, all instincts of any high degree of development involve a combination of many such acts. Instincts may also be served by intelligence, in which case we do not speak of them as pure, but at the point at which intelligence is able to grasp the entire trend of action, to foresee the end, and determine the means freely without reference to any hereditary propensity to a specific form of approach, we pass out of the region of instinct and enter that of intelligent purpose."[4] Upon this level of behavior the *primary correlation* taking place is that of race experience. A useful instinct beginning to develop in an animal gives it an advantage in the struggle for existence and, presumably, each increment added to the instinct brings an added increment of survival value to its possessor. Fluctuations in the direction of positive disadvantage in the struggle to survive are of course a disadvantage and possessors of such fluctuations tend to pass out of the picture. Thus we may speak of instincts as being a result of the correlation of racial experience. Do lower animals have any other methods of correlating experience? Mr. Hobhouse holds that they have many other methods; he carried out extensive experiments with animals to see just how much intelligence could be attributed to them.

The famous experiments of Hobhouse to determine the intelligence of certain animals, widely and favorably commented upon at the time of their first publication, show us what progress has been made during a quarter century in establishing objective criteria for controlled experimentation. Thus we observe that the time of the experiment was not regularly taken, and the personal attitude of the experimenter was allowed to enter into the interpretation of results to a surprising degree. Regarding an experiment per-

[4] *Mind in Evolution*, pp. 105-106.

formed with an unfamiliar cat he states, "From what I saw of the cat, I am more inclined to think that there was not much discrimination between clawing at the meat and clawing the jug over."[5]

The experiments could hardly be spoken of as "controlled" even by the most lenient critic of today. Of an experiment with his dog he states, "Jack never showed any appreciation of the mechanism of this arrangement, for after he had learned to push at the door, he frequently came to the wrong side. I must admit, however, that by pushing hard enough on the wrong side he caused the door to rebound, and so on several occasions obtained his desire."[6] Again, a dog is charged with failure in a trick involving the placing of a weight in a basket, his reward being food. Yet the dog secured his food through the unprescribed method of putting his paws into the basket and thus pushing it down. The poor beast was probably entirely unaware of his failure to solve the food-getting problem.[7] Experiments, it seems, rarely took place under identical conditions. Thus, "I did not give him the slightest hint or reminder, but after he had waited stupidly for a long time, I told him to go on, in the reproachful tone which one might use to a person who really knows a thing, but is suffering from some inhibition which prevents his using it. In Jack's case my remarks seemed precisely to have this effect of removing the inhibition, or perhaps of supplying the needed stimulus to set the machinery to work."[8]

The actual tests included several forms of puzzle-boxes, pulling strings, opening drawers, upsetting jugs etc.,—all with the urge of a hungry animal for food as

[5] *Ibid.*, p. 210.
[6] *Ibid.*, p. 217.
[7] *Ibid.*, p. 219.
[8] *Ibid.*, p. 228.

the motivating force. Did the animals solve these problems entirely as a result of random motions, which when successful tended to be repeated more quickly at the next attempt until the animal was completely habituated to the right process, or was something else involved? For Hobhouse there was most emphatically something else. There was in certain instances clear evidence of learning though "perception of results" to follow from a given act.[9]

In this position regarding animal intelligence Hobhouse differs sharply from Thorndike and the full extent of these differences and the reasons therefor are argued by him in great detail. His main conclusions follow: the animal learns most easily where the first act is his own and the second a result of that act which gratifies or hurts him; the animal often has a "practical idea" (direction of action to an external change) and this practical idea is correlated with a remote end, forming thus a "practical judgment"; animal perception, however, is crude when compared with human perception, and the ideas correspondingly crude; there is no natural tendency to learn by perception or by reflective imitation. Finally the writer concludes that there is no essential difference in the learning ability of dogs, cats, elephants, and monkeys so far as his tests revealed. He found greater differences between individual dogs than between a dog and an elephant. His studies were not confined to his own observations but an extensive range of materials in animal psychology was considered.

It is curiously true that he found it necessary to discuss in meticulous detail the claim of the Elberfeld

[9] In this view Hobhouse is in approximate agreement with the Gestalt theory of which so much has been written in psychology of late. See especially: *The Mentality of Apes* by Wolfgang Kohler. Harcourt Brace, 1925. Based on experiments ending in 1917 and first published in that year.

Horses and regretted his inability to make personal observations of their prowess. These amazing animals, it would seem, were mathematicians of no mean ability. One horse gave at a glance the correct answer to the problem: $\sqrt[4]{2825761} - \sqrt[4]{531441} = $ ————. In a fifteen page discussion of the matter Hobhouse concludes that the animals had no such ability as was imputed to them.[10]

So much for the "upper limit" of animal intelligence. Hobhouse has at least a receptive mind toward any suggestion which would indefinitely advance the usually accepted terminal point; and his own limit is much higher than that generally accepted by other psychologists. One may be allowed to observe in this connection that in a sketch of the significance of mind in evolution any proven advance in animal intelligence enhances by so much the significance of mind in the struggle for existence.

The discussion up to this point has carried us through reflex, instinct, and an examination of experiments conducted by the author and others. We have now to consider Hobhouse's logical analysis of advancing stages of intelligence.

"Experience"—that contact with a varying environment on which inference is founded, is the basis of the higher organism's assimilation of its environment and adjustment to it. Assimilation involves a selective modification of conduct. The stentor persistently stimulated varies its reactions until a satisfying one results. If later the same stimulus is applied, the previously satisfying reaction is more quickly given. Assimilation is aided through confirmation and inhibition. The reaction that has once brought painful results is inhibited; the one that brought satisfaction is repeated or confirmed.

[10] *Ibid.*, pp. 447-462.

Thus the pain felt in connection with undesirable stimuli is the expression in consciousness of inhibitory movements, as of withdrawal, flight, or rejection. Pleasure is the expression of confirmatory movements tending to prolong and bring a repetition of the action. All of which does not necessitate ideas but is Primary Retentiveness. The crab has Primary Retentiveness when it holds the image of the sand hopper while it goes about the slow process of stalking and capturing it. *Experience* has the general function of increasing plasticity, thereby assisting instinctive reaction patterns to adjust to a varying environment. Intelligence upon this level is widely diffused throughout the animal world. Witness the homing tendency of fish. The shark returns to favorable hunting grounds. Among invertebrates, learning by experience is to be found among many insects, spiders, and crustacea. For the last type Hobhouse cites an instance of a snail dropped into a tank previously occupied by it and immediately finding its way to the surface.

What is the next type of intelligence to be observed in the gradual rise of mind in the evolutionary process? Hobhouse puts down "practical judgment,"—a judgment involving ideas and a clear notion of relationships based on revival of concrete experiences. A mind in which only very definite and tangible ideas flow may on seeing one side of a house recall where the door is located on the opposite side and direct conduct accordingly. This is less than analytic thought for the distinct relationships are not dissected out as elements in consciousness. With the practical judgment comes a knowledge of objects,—the "object" being a kind of structure involving related elements. The practical judgment makes possible memory and anticipation.

With the rise of practical judgment comes the change in mental evolution most momentous for Hobhouse,—

the possibility for the first time of purposive conduct. Without consciousness, purposive action is impossible. As long as *habit* is dominant we have adaptive action, but when action is based on the relation between the thing done and the result of doing it, we have purpose. "Every act which the purposive state of mind dictates is done because of its causal relation to the final result."[11] We may be sure that any action is purposive if the relation on which it is based may be experienced without leading to the formation of a habit and if it may be applied in circumstances differing from those in which it was originally perceived. "Action would seem to be the primitive and natural accompaniment of an idea and it is only in the course of further evolution that ideas arise which do not prompt to action."[12]

With the development of practical judgment comes the possibility of thinking of objects as *wholes,* and of forming a higher *correlation* of experience than had been possible previously. Learning through practical judgment based on concrete experience has advantages over assimilation: only one experience is required as a basis of future action, and the results of experience are applied to action in a manner not determined by the experience itself. So it comes about that the correlations based on the practical judgment are those of "articulate complexes." Such correlation is similar to the stage of logical procedure where one reasons from particulars to particulars and where the implied universal is not made explicit. This form of correlation Hobhouse, on the basis of his own experiments, believes to exist among the higher animals.

Attention is directed to the fact that higher animals have a knowledge of individuals, going beyond a mere mechanical reaction to customary stimuli. This is not-

[11] *Ibid.,* p. 163.
[12] *Ibid.,* p. 166.

ably true of the ape, dog, and elephant. Also, animals
show ability to use with discrimination past experience. Observe the pointer running around the game
and driving it toward the hunter. Can we, however,
ascribe to an animal the articulate idea, *i.e.,* "one in
which comparatively distinct elements are held in comparatively distinct relations"? Hobhouse holds that this
can be done with certain apes. He quotes a number
of puzzle-solving problems carried out under his direction and these established the point to his mind. The
experiments were carried out with the same lack of
laboratory technique as was previously noted.

The sketch of mental development before the level
of *homo sapiens* is reached has now been completed,
for Hobhouse does not maintain that animals go beyond relatively simple "articulate ideas." We have seen
the source of this writer's interest in the course of
mental evolution to lie in the philosophical problem
of Mind *vs.* Mechanism. We have seen the philosopher
invade the field of animal psychology and perform
many ingenious experiments but without the "controls" now universally accepted as necessary for a scientific study of animal behavior. Finally we have followed
through his logical classification of stages of mentality
from its elementary stages to the articulate ideas of
the ape. In epitome, then, there lies before us the basis
of later studies relating to man's freedom from ma-
chanism and his moral responsibility. This is a fundamental problem for Hobhouse and one treated by him
in great detail. It is a little to one side of the main
purpose of this volume as it lies more in the realm of
philosophy than of social theory. Of greater interest
to us is his sketch of social evolution, both historically
and as to its psychological basis; his penetrating studies
in social ethics, and his general views of the field of
sociology.

III. THE BROAD LINES OF SOCIAL EVOLUTION

1. Introductory

A deal of scholarship and a vast amount of research have enabled Hobhouse to set out what he conceives to be the main lines of social evolution. For the later years of his sketch he can draw upon the written records extending from ancient Egypt and Babylonia to the present day. This he has done with skill. For the earlier years he is hard put to it since archaeology gives only the scantiest material. He has turned, therefore, to an elaborate consideration of the primitive people of today. In his *Morals in Evolution* (1923) and especially in *The Material Culture and Social Institutions of the Simpler People* (written in collaboration with G. C. Wheeler and Mr. Ginsberg) he has dealt at length with information drawn from the ethnologists' descriptions of the "Simpler People." While there is much that is illuminating and of value in this work Hobhouse has allowed himself to slip into certain errors difficult to avoid in using the comparative method,—a method extensively employed by Westermarck in analyzing primitive society.

A few general examples of the comparative method will clarify a somewhat technical discussion. The great weakness of this comparative method lies in its tendency to take facts out of their natural setting involved to high degree or reduced to simplest ele- and consequently give them a wholly erroneous inter- pretation. The life of a society, be it complicated and ments, presents a unit to be understood as a unit. Whether the interest lies in methods of administering justice, or marriage taboos, the bare facts in the case are deceptive and meaningless apart from the setting in which they occur. Many students of primitive peoples have set down with care a particular fact observed, especially if it has certain bizarre elements. Boas reports that in the northwest on the Pacific Coast a certain song apparently praising an unknown goddess was recorded. It might have been carefully put down by ethnologists to be used in studying the religious beliefs of these tribes. Further contact with the people who sang it showed it to be a satirical song devised to sting out of her complacency a girl who had offended the group.

First contact with certain Central Australians brought out the astonishing fact that they could not count beyond five. Surely conclusive proof of native mental incapacity. Yet further observation showed that the native had little difficulty in learning more advanced arithmetic. His normal mode of existence made no demand for the higher mathematics and he had not developed it. It is probably unnecessary to state that Hobhouse did not fall into any such obvious errors as those just indicated, but they indicate something of the dangers of the comparative method.

After gathering a vast amount of material Hobhouse and his associates proceed to analyze it with a view to discovering whether any relationship exists between methods of food-getting and the non-material social institutions. This is a study of such importance that its methodology deserves analysis in some detail. He has used its results extensively in his other writings.

Primitive people he divides into seven groups: lower hunters, higher hunters, lower pastoral, higher pastoral, lower agriculturalists, middle agriculturalists, higher agriculturalists. These classes are abbreviated H_1, H_2, P_1, P_2, A_1, A_2, A_3. Stages in the development of such an institution as marriage are compared with these economic stages. Certain grave difficulties arise. Great care is used in setting down the objective criteria by which it is determined that a particular group shall be classed as A_1 rather than A_2 yet from the very nature of the material it is inevitable that marginial cases require treatment in a somewhat arbitrary way. Another ethnologist might well classify certain groups differently. The error here is slight, however, compared to the difficulty of defining the statistical unit to be used in compiling the results. The various designations for groups of peoples—clan, tribe, phratry, etc., are used so differently by different ethnologists that it would be impossible to carry through a uniform statistical unit on the basis of a uniform nomenclature. Here Hobhouse has done the obviously common-sense thing; he has treated the unit as set down and described by the ethnologist in each case. Yet this opens wide the door to very serious errors. The unit varies greatly in size and in the number of sub-units that it may contain. The skewed results likely to occur from a statistical treatment of such material are obvious. Hobhouse gives it as his opinion that errors here tend to cancel one another. Perhaps so. Yet the theory of compensating errors seems to provide a doubtful foundation on which to erect this statistical structure. The number of cases is relatively small.

Another methodological difficulty arises in the field of interpretation. One of the commonplaces of ethnological study relates to the ease with which certain traits of one group will be imitated and adopted by another group. *Diffusion* is a widely observed phenomenon. Regarding this difficulty Hobhouse states: "If an institution has, in fact, propagated and maintained itself over a great area, even though its origin be in some unitary cause, we cannot regard its extensive prevalence as unimportant or insignificant."[1] Yes; diffusion *is* highly significant, and so also is the correlation of material culture and social institution, yet these are two distinct things. Let us take an hypothetical case. An observer states that over a certain vast area the same methods prevail for settling internal disputes, due evidently to diffusion; also in this area, similar methods of food getting are to be found, again due to diffusion. If then in our hypothetical area fifteen cases are reported and meticulously tabulated under appropriate heading of First Agricultural and Dispute Settled by Tribal Council do we in fact have fifteen cases to tabulate or one? It seems evident that in the long list of peoples studied by Hobhouse and his associates there are two obvious groupings, the Malay Archipelago and Central Africa. This gives some point to the hypothetical objection just raised.

Finally, it is to be observed that the non-material culture of a people may be related to many things other than methods of food-getting. Thus in the field of judicial administration it is obvious that the amount of social control necessary varies somewhat with the density of population. Due consideration to facts of this type apparently have not been given.

In conclusion, then, it seems clear that the Hobousian method of studying the early stages of social evolution is to be called in question. The comparative method of treating ethnological material, difficulties of classifying cases and defining the statistical unit, the problem of diffusion, and various disturbing factors such as variation in density of population,—all combine to raise doubts as to the validity of the results obtained. It is only just to indicate that Hobhouse was aware of most of these difficulties, notably

[1] *The Material Culture and Social Institutions of the Simpler People,* p. 11.

the problem of defining the statistical unit. He gives cautions in regard to drawing sweeping conclusions. It must also be said, however, that he has elsewhere extensively used his own study and not always with the same caution he advises in others. This is especially true in the later editions of *Morals in Evolution*.

It will be evident in the following paragraphs, as we run through the author's sketch of the main aspects of social evolution, which sections have been compiled from ethnological sources in the manner indicated and which from recognized historic sources.

For the purposes of clarity the evolution of different phases of community life are sketched successively. The aspects here considered are: law and justice, the position of women, inter-community relations, inter-class relations, and economic relations.[2]

2. *Law and Justice*

As regards law and justice and the various methods by which it is or is not obtained, Hobhouse believes that certain discernible trends are to be observed from the lower hunters of primitive society to the great nations of today. There are, he indicates, two lines of evolution in law and justice: either the method of self-redress may be organized and reduced to a regular system, or the maintenance of order and redress of wrongs may take place by the community acting through its chief men, this leading naturally to a regularly constituted organ to administer justice. These two lines of evolution are considered separately though in point of fact they are intertwined. There follows a summary of Hobhouse's views on the evolution of law and justice.

Vengeance is a system which is less heard of among the most primitive peoples than among those slightly

[2] *Morals in Evolution*, especially pp. 1-354.

higher in development. As it grows, we have redress gained by retaliation, and through the solidarity of the family the sufferer finds support from it in seeking redress. Thus vengeance grows to be the blood feud. Later *lex talionis* develops and is certainly found as early as the Code of Hammurabi.

As a fairly early stage in developing judicial procedure the principle of payment for damages makes its appearance. It is peculiarly characteristic of the settling down of barbarous tribes into a peaceful and relatively civilized life. Quite naturally it is here that distinctions of rank, age, and sex appear. Furthermore one observes that primitive man often will not assist his near neighbor in a fight. This is because it would involve him and his group in a permanent feud, and fear of this acts as one of the great restraints in primitive society. In the feud the whole family of the offender may be destroyed with him. Among the head hunting tribes common in southeastern Asia collective responsibility is carried so far that the head of a woman or child is considered as valuable as that of a warrior.

"With the theory of collective responsibility goes almost necessarily the failure to distinguish between accident and design. . . . The whole distinction between design and accident is by no means so clear to the primitive man as it is to us . . . the nascent reflection of the savage is strangled at birth by the prevailing theory of witchcraft and possession."[3] The primitive man oftentimes punished animals or even inanimate objects and it naturally followed that responsibility was inadequately defined in the case of idiots and minors. The principle of collective responsibility continues to a late date; in France down to the time of the Revolution the whole family was made

[3] *Ibid.,* pp. 83-84.

to suffer with the person who had committed a political crime.

As centralized authority developed the administration of justice became more of an orderly public function. In its growth several lines are discernable. Probably the earliest public offences to be publicly punished were those against the firmly established taboos of the group. Such apparently trivial things as mistakes in dancing, as among the Bella Coola and Salish, lead to group punishment, the object of punishment being the removal of the curse from the community. Again we observe in the developing public justice that there are occasional explosions of popular sympathy for someone manifestly abused, but such explosions are of course unregulated. However, to prevent the dreaded blood feud, chiefs or others may take steps to settle the quarrel in its early stages through some form of adjustment.

One common modification of crude self-redress is the set fight. These run the entire gamut of variation,— from an innocuous affair to one ending in death. Further, an injured man may obtain on occasion direct assistance from his chief or from the community in securing redress for injury. In rarer instances the chief directs pursuit of the culprit and inflicts the punishment,—but this involves only retaliation. Again it is observed that both *atonement* and *composition* are widely used among the simpler peoples of today as forms of settlement for offences committed. *Atonement* is a settlement either with group, or god, or conscience; it is of wider application than *composition,* which involves direct payment to the relatives through a public award.

Public control of the judicial process is important, however, even under a system of blood revenge, for the more keenly the wider group sympathizes with the avenger of blood the easier it is for him to carry through his object. Often a public council is held after some grave offence has been committed and both accuser and accused tell their stories. The council may then pass sentence but take no effective action to carry it out. Here the court is peacemaker rather than judge and this constitutes a transition stage in the development of judicial procedure. Yet the primitive group, with its ability to ostracize and drive out of the community anyone who outrages public feeling, had a potent instrument of social control which could be shaped later into an orderly judicial procedure. However, even after an orderly method of administering justice has been worked out within a tribe or smaller group there may be complete absence of judicial procedure for inter-group offences. This is notably true of the Central Australians.

In this way, then, does Hobhouse picture the early stages in the development of judicial procedure. He visualizes three broad stages: first, self-redress with or without composition. Second, the avenger is assisted or controlled by the public. (Here are included cases in which murder and grave offences are publicly punished, also cases in which a judicial system is well established but private redress is allowed.) Third, public judicial system deals with grave offences in a regular and well-established manner.

The question then arises, if primitive peoples of whom we have accurate records are arranged according to the development of their material culture especially on the basis of food-getting habits, is there any relation between these habits and their form of judicial procedure? Hobhouse believes there is an important relation between the two. He states: "When we compare these three grades of judicial procedure with our economic classification we find (1) a continuous increase of public justice from the lower hunters

to the higher pastorals and (2) in self-redress a corresponding descent from the higher hunters to the highest agriculturalists, but the lower hunters do not show
so high a percentage as the higher hunters. . . ."[4] The
caution with which this position can be taken has been
touched upon previously. The comparative and statistical method of treating ethnological material leaves
much to be desired.

Turning from ethnology to recorded history there is
abundant evidence of a transition from private to
public justice. Ancient Egypt is the exception; here
even political offenders were brought to trial. However,
in all the other codes of the ancients there is evidence
of an original private system of justice. The distinction between private and public offences is at the foundation of Roman law, and the rebarbarization of
Europe in the Early Middle Ages is vividly shown by
the breakdown of the system of public justice. Historic
Greece had a fully developed system of public justice.
There was no criminal process for unintentional offences and the whole legal procedure was intelligently
organized.

From the theoretical stand-point judicial procedure
leads to an interesting observation. The community with
better order obviously has enhanced thereby its possibilities of survival, and it is likely that the primitive
hunters and agriculturalists of today are better gov-
erned than were people with similar modes of livelihood
centuries ago. "We may infer that if we could see the
ascending scale of society set out in time as we see it
through anthropology at what is (relatively to the duration of human society) a single moment, the correlation of the methods of justice with the general advance
of civilization would be not less close but closer than

[4] *Ibid.,* p. 105.

that which we have seen."[5] Public justice grows not
out of vengeance (for many simple societies do not
operate a revenge system) but out of a common desire
for safety and order. True justice comes through the
fusion of a conception of the welfare of the community
and of a feeling of pity for the guilty person.

Obviously, society has gone only a short way toward
securing justice when it establishes public courts to
decide issues in dispute; the next step consists of working out a rational procedure for getting the facts in the
dispute and coming to a decision upon them. The
"oath" and "judicial combat" in time are replaced by
the "ordeal," where heaven is called upon at once to
show where justice lies. Furthermore it is only when
the executive power of government has sufficient force
to prevent revenge being taken upon the officer administering it that true public justice can come into being.
It follows also that when kindred are no longer allowed
to take vengeance, the right of the offender to make
peace with the kin is also withdrawn; crime becomes a
public matter to be dealt with by state authority. The
old idea of vengeance breaks up into punishment inflicted by the judge and restitution assigned to the com-
plainant. So today civil and criminal justice are distinct. Historically, even after torture as a means of securing evidence has been abolished, the accused is still
under handicap, for in giving evidence and calling
witnesses he is much restricted. Even today, Hobhouse
maintains, something of the old combat idea remains in
the court trial; possibly our descendants will smile at a
system that allows the person with greatest means to
secure the best legal counsel.

Public justice in early times was severe in obtaining
proof, but even more in punishment. Thus in early England death was theoretically possible as punishment for

[5] *Ibid.*, pp. 113-114.

all felonies. In the 18th century women were still burned alive for such offences as murder of husband or master, and both men and women were whipped for small offences. Prisons were a great scandal. "Gaol-fever raged, prisons were still private property, and the prisoner, innocent or guilty, had to fee his gaoler and pay for every comfort and even for necessaries. In the Bishop of Ely's prison the gaoler prevented escapes by chaining his prisoners on their backs on the floor, and fastening a spiked iron collar about their necks."[6]

As substitutes for the old savagery there grew up the custom of transporting the prisoner to some other country to give him a fresh start. Later the penitentiary made its appearance. Much remains to be done in regard to the humane treatment of prisoners. "Its dealings with the criminal mark, one may say, the zero point in the scale of treatment which society conceives to be the due of its various members. If we raise this point we raise the standard all along the scale."[7] For the pauper, the worker, and others in inferior positions may expect better treatment than the criminal. The plan of turning a man loose upon society more hardened and hopeless than when he was taken into custody is quite unjustifiable.

The history of human law and justice up to the present time and the natural lines of its growth as visualized in broad outline in the Hobhousian scheme are now clear. His own summary follows. "Briefly to resume the main phases in the evolution of public justice, we find that at the outset pure anarchy or self-redress is qualified first by the sense of solidarity within the primary social unit. This expresses itself first in the repression of offences, especially of a sacral char-

[6] *Ibid.*, p. 124.
[7] *Ibid.*, p. 125.

acter, held dangerous to the group as a whole, and then in the control of self-redress. As between the primary units a system of collective self-redress arises which in turn yields to the authority of chief or council representing the larger community as a whole. As long as the vindication of rights rests mainly in the hands of the kindred or other group, responsibility is collective, intention is apt to be ignored and punishment is not assessed according to the merit of the individual. When retaliation is mitigated by the introduction of money payments no change in ethical principle occurs. It is only as social order evolves an independent organ for the adjustment of disputes and the prevention of crime, that the ethical idea becomes separated out from the conflicting passions which are its earlier husk, and step by step the individual is separated from his family, his intentions are taken into account, his formal rectitude or want of rectitude is thrown into the background by the essential justice of the case, appeals to magical processes are abandoned, and the law sets before itself the aim of discovering the facts and maintaining right or punishing wrong accordingly.

"The rise of public justice proper necessitates the gradual abandonment of the whole conception of the trial as a struggle between two parties, and substitutes the idea of ascertaining the actual truth in order that justice may be done. That is at first carried out by supernatural means, viz., by the Ordeal and the Oath. These in turn give way to a true judicial inquiry by evidence and rational proof."[8]

3. The Position of Women and Marriage

The next important phase of social evolution to which Hobhouse gives attention is marriage and the

[8] *Ibid.*, p. 131.

position of women. He points out certain trends held to be distinct ethical gains. The problem breaks itself naturally into several parts and consideration is first given to the *form* of marriage.

Whether group marriage has ever existed is doubtful: in some cases the husband has only a preferential control over his wife, as among certain Central Australians. Regarding polygamy, the most important ethical question is whether it is *allowed* under any circumstances whatever, and not its extent. Among primitive people in the lower economic grades, according to the classification previously discussed, it is most widely found but it is also extensive in higher grades, especially among the pastoral peoples. Wealth conditions the amount of polygamy to be observed. By contrast polyandry is rather exceptional. It is due primarily to poverty and lack of women. In higher civilizations monogamy becomes well-nigh universal and the family becomes more close-knit. However, all along the scale certain impediments to marriage arise.

In the simpler societies laws of exogamy and endogamy, bewildering in variety and extent, present serious obstacles to a union. In general, they tend to bar the marriage bond where another bond already exists,— such as blood kinship. Violation of a rule of exogamy is regarded with horror. Yet in spite of its binding nature exogamy performs certain functions with fair constancy: it checks extreme in-breeding; it binds distinct groups together; and it has an ethical function. This latter is seen in the regulations of what Hobhouse calls the "instinctive" incest horror. Psychologically considered extreme regulations of the exogamic type are to be understood through mother-child attachment and horror of any violation of its sacred character. It grows out of an unduly extended taboo and an insufficient understanding of blood relationships.

Civilized ethics makes free mating easier as regards kinship. The stability of the marriage relationship presents a different picture.

Divorce may take a bewildering variety of forms among primitive as well as among civilized peoples. It may be perfectly free to either partner or free to both by mutual consent; or free to the husband or the wife; it may be free on consent of the family; or it may be wholly forbidden. Where the payment of some valuable article is required to secure divorce it tends to make the marriage state more permanent. Again drawing upon ethnological material, treated in his usual comparative and statistical method, and based upon his own *Simpler Peoples,* Hobhouse concludes that among the primitive people marriage is dissolved at the will of either party in seven groups out of every ten. Closely related to divorce are the methods by which marriage is brought about in any group.

Marriage may be arranged through capture, or "consideration rendered," or mutual consent. Marriage by capture is a genuine if relatively rare method. The more ordinary procedure in obtaining the bride is either by true purchase, the bride being a chattel, or by modified purchase, where the gifts made to the bride's parents constitute true compensation, but are given in keeping with the dignity of the bride. Oftentimes the gifts of the husband or his family may be balanced or exceeded by the gifts of the bride's family. At other times the husband renders certain services to the bride's family. The method of exchange, whereby the girl in one family is exchanged for one in another, not infrequently obtains.

Great varieties of marriage through consent also exist. Abduction is generally illicit, yet extremely common, and punishment of it tends to resolve itself into formal expiation. With the family once established, several relations are possible between husband and wife.

The internal structure of the family may vary from tyrannous control by one member to mutual understanding and respect. Oftentimes the "natural family" of husband and wife and children is not complete—as when the maternal clan system interferes, or it may be complete with the husband as ruler, this through the subjection of the wife, or we may have marriage maintained by the closest moral bond, with full respect for the personality of each member. This last form is not yet widely realized; it is a problem which civilization has yet to solve. Among the simpler peoples what is common is not the organized matriarchate (rule by women) but "mother-right," and here, paradoxically, the situation of the woman may be extremely bad, for the head of the family is often the mother's brother.

Historically, the family has, of course, known a bewildering variety of forms; Hobhouse makes a significant generalization. "In all Indo-Germanic peoples, among Semites and Mongolians, in a word, among all races who have developed a historic civilization, father right predominates. Thus, broadly, when we contrast the civilized with the uncivilized world, we find mother-right confined to the latter, and within it we find it relatively most frequent in the lower cultures."[9] The rise of the paternal family is conditioned by the recognition of paternity. This often carries with it a curious custom, the couvade,—the husband going to bed prior to child-birth and receiving every consideration from the community while the wife goes about her tasks as usual. The paternal family may also arise through forms of marriage involving the appropriation of the woman. Where the patriarchate (rule by men)

[9] *Ibid.,* p. 162.

is strongly developed purchase or quasi-purchase of the wife is often found. There are a few cases among the primitive people where woman's footing is equal to man's but these are the exception. Thus, even where divorce is freely granted to either party it works to the disadvantage of the woman who is more interested in maintaining the tie. The woman is generally the *property* of her husband or guardian, hence the widespread practice of wife lending. The claim to fidelity is usually one-sided and the father may often devote his daughter to prostitution,—religious or otherwise. The question arises, would it be possible to reach general conclusions regarding the relative unfavorableness in the position of woman in primitive society? Hobhouse makes an attempt in this direction. He adds a system of point scoring to his already familiar comparative and statistical treatment of ethnological material.

In this attempt objectively to rate the position of women among the simpler peoples the problem of which is *the better* of two situations is often raised; Hobhouse deals with this question variously. For example, monogamy is regarded as favorable, polygamy as unfavorable, because civilized women would so regard these customs. A summary of the scores for various primitive people, grouped as hunters, pastorals, and agriculturalists, shows the position of women generally to be unfavorable. The point scores show the proportion of groups in which the position of woman is clearly bad to be: pastorals, eighty-seven per cent; hunters, eighty-two per cent; agriculturalists, seventy-three per cent.

In any society there is a constant tug of war between the forces working to elevate the position of woman and those tending to lower it. However, until such time as the ethical factor comes into prominence, Hobhouse indicates, woman's life is bitter and hard. The advantage lies with man and his superior physical strength. Beginnings of this ethical factor can be seen in the legal codes of earliest civilizations.

A glimpse at the position of woman with the dawn of written history in the important nations of the world gives interesting if contradictory pictures. The patriarchal family was established as the primary social unit. In the early civilizations of Asia the position of women was bad; under the code of Hammurabi marriage was arranged by the parents; commercial considerations dominated the law of divorce. In later Asiatic civilizations polygamy appears, though in restricted form. Early Babylonian society permitted woman to conduct business, under restrictions, and later woman could protect herself against the possibility of a second wife putting in her appearance. This was done by the canny arrangement of writing pecuniary penalties into the marriage contract. In ancient Egypt great obscurity surrounds the position of woman; however, from the Old Kingdom onward woman had full rights of property and could go to law. Under contract, barring polygamy and arranged at the time of marriage, divorce could be obtained, yet these contracts applied only to the propertied classes. Concubinage was frequent, brother and sister marriages not rare. One of the early moralists of Egypt indicates that a man who loves his wife should "fill her stomach and clothe her back."[10] It later developed that woman took an important part in industrial and commercial life, talked freely with men, did manual labor, and carried on trade publicly.

What of the position of woman in early India? The tradition of the *Vedas* shows paternal power fully developed; the daughter might even be sold outright to an intended husband, and traces of a previously existing polygamy are shown. A woman was permitted, if her

[10] Quoted, *ibid.,* p. 185.

father failed to secure a husband within three years after she reached maturity, to marry as she wished. Once married her husband must be worshipped as a god. If the wife committed faults she might be beaten, with a rope or split bamboo, but only on the back, never on the noble parts. The Brahmans, believing woman's disposition to be evil, tactfully recommend that the wife be kept busy in the house. According to the strict theory of Manu, whose early mythological code still shapes much of Indian thought, a wife should have no property, though this was often violated. The Code provides further that, "A barren wife may be superseded in the eighth year, she whose children all die in the tenth, she who bares only daughters in the eleventh, but she who is quarrelsome without delay."[11] Woman is never a free agent. Children were highly regarded and it was not unusual for a childless husband to force his wife to bare a child by another man.

Turning to China, it is indicated that there has been no fundamental change in the position of woman during the historic period. Marriage is arranged by parents, but this applies to son as well as daughter. For any one man the full ceremony of marriage is performed with only one woman, but there may be several concubines. These must obey the wife, and she is forbidden to be jealous of them. A husband may kill his wife taken in adultery; on other occasions he may strike her without wounding her. If she retaliates and strikes him she is publicly punished with one hundred blows. The divorce law favors man. The great teachers did nothing to elevate the position of woman. Mencius quotes with approval the three obediences for a woman; when young she obeys her parents, when married her husband, when widowed her son. In the *She-King* it is

[11] Quoted, *ibid.*, p. 191, from Manu.

stated: "Disorder does not come down from heaven, it is produced by the woman. Those from whom come no lesson, no instruction, are women and eunuchs."[12] It may be remarked, parenthetically, that coming out of such a background it would not be surprising to find the "woman's movement" of today going to excesses in China, just as it would not have been surprising among the ancient Hebrews.

The record of Hebrew marriage begins with the patriarchal family fully developed. Wife by purchase or service was the rule. Polygamy, concubinage, sale of a daughter are allowed. By the time of the *Proverbs,* however, monogamy is assumed by the writers. Woman is usually thought of as a source of evil. Hobhouse summarizes: "A bad woman is the temptress and the destroyer throughout the Wisdom literature, and it was through woman that sin came into the world, and for this reason, that she was to be subject to her husband."[13] In contrast with the Mohammedan world the position of woman steadily advanced among the Hebrews.

Among the Arabs of Mohammed's time women were mere chattels. Certain sayings,—"Women are the whips of Satan," "A man can bear anything but the mention of his wives"—indicate the attitude. Mohammed attempted to ameliorate the position of woman yet we would hardly characterize him as a fanatical reformer. He limited the number of wives to four with concubinage unlimited. He tolerated free divorce, but the wife was protected by the bride price, a portion of which was returned on divorce without cause. Here her position reminds one of the Babylonian and Egyptian woman possessed of her marriage contract. Mohammed mildly remonstrates: "Not one of you must whip his

[12] *Ibid.,* p. 197, from the *She-King.*
[13] *Ibid.,* p. 200.

wife like whipping a slave"; and, "Admonish your wives with kindness because women were created from the crooked bone of the side."[14] The Mohammedans are in line with a great body of strictly male traditions which regard woman as both a blessing and a curse. Thus at the opposite pole from the sayings just quoted, "The world and all things in it are valuable, but more valuable than all is a virtuous woman."[15] Hence the Mohammedan woman is secluded for two reasons, as a compliment and as a precaution. How different from the conventionally accepted view of ancient Greece where the smile of a beautiful Helen was as devastating as a whole army of mere fighting *men*.

The Greeks of Homer's time contemplated one legitimate wife; if she could not be taken in a raid she was purchased with cattle or other valued articles. Over his concubines a man had the power of life and death. In historic times the father was the religious and legal head of the family; the sons divided the inheritance; the daughter received maintenance and a dowry. However, such property as women had remained theirs during marriage, and in some states they had the right to manage their own property. In Athens, woman could be divorced on repayment of the bride price; at Sparta, looser relations prevailed. Here brother might share his wife with brother, and wife lending was a recognized custom. Yet woman was more than a chattel even in Sparta. The classic philosophers were mildly interested in woman's betterment. Aristotle held that woman should be ruled as a magistrate rules a free state. Plato, more liberal, stressed woman's duties rather than her rights; he insisted on the loss which the state sustained in keeping her restricted within the family circle. Aristotle thought woman possessed

[14] *Ibid.*, p. 201.
[15] *Ibid.*, p. 202.

slight deliberative ability, which is not strange since there were no regular schools for girls at Athens. The ideal wife, for many of the philosophers, is a good housekeeper. There are many similarities between the early Greek and Roman views of woman's place in the world and her duties.

Roman history begins with paternal power developed as completely as it has existed anywhere in the world. However, only one wife was permitted and divorce was almost impossible to secure. After the time of the Twelve Tables a new type of marriage developed rapidly and undermined both the stability of the marriage relation and the autocratic power of the husband. By a legal fiction, if cohabitation were broken three nights in the year the wife did not become the property of her husband; she remained under the nominal control of her father but was in reality a free agent. She controlled her own property and, to considerable extent, her own person. "Hence the Roman matron of the Empire was more fully her own mistress than the married woman of any earlier civilization, with the possible exception of a certain period of Egyptian history, and, it must be added, than the wife of any later civilization down to our own generation."[16] During this period of the later empire divorce was granted freely at the choice of either party. Whether this had a demoralizing effect upon the empire is a matter on which the authorities strongly disagree. The Roman matron evidently was her husband's companion, counsellor, and friend, much as she had been under more rigorous marriage laws.

"The modern European marriage law has three roots, Roman law, primitive Teutonic custom, and the Christian doctrine of marriage; but it has been largely re-

[16] *Ibid.,* p. 209.

modelled in the modern period under rationalizing in-
fluences."[17] In the Middle Ages the Roman marriage
law made contact with primitive Germanic customs
where also father-right was fully developed. The church
regarded marriage as a concession to the weakness
of the flesh. The chief concern of the church was to
prevent the deadly sin of fornication and this resulted
in marriage being reduced to the simplest possible
terms. Finally the church brought about the tradition
that the consent of the two parties was the only necessary condition to a valid marriage. The result of this
is important for it emancipated women of both servile
and free classes regarding the most important event in
their lives. However, it follows also from the church's
position that marriage is indissoluble,—though of
course it might be annulled by simply declaring it never
had existed. It also follows from the tradition of the
church that violation of the marriage law affected man
as well as woman, and this was an ethical departure of
the greatest importance. These positions of the church
were only established upon the frail and imperfect basis
that human nature allows after long struggle with the
people under their control. Advance in woman's position has always come slowly and left a vast deal to be
desired even in European countries at comparatively
recent dates.

In the middle of the modern period, at the time of
Blackstone, woman had practically no legal personality;
at law she was absorbed in her husband. Yet this position was combatted both by religion and by the growing romantic attitude toward woman and marriage.
Witness the great mass of verse written "To My
Lady's Eyebrow." The leaders of the Reformation,
feeling the stirring of the times, declined to regard

[17] *Ibid.*, p. 206.

marriage either as a sacrament or as a concession to the weakness of the flesh. However, Old Testament notions of the patriarchal family were strongly entrenched and not until the nineteenth century, even in Protestant countries, did important legislation begin to take shape and fundamentally change the position of woman. In England this did not occur until the Married Woman's Property Act of 1870 and 1882. Since then there have been many changes.

The tendency of modern marriage laws is to guarantee to the wife equality of civil status, but the effects of these laws upon the permanence of the marriage tie are various. "Countries which have maintained the rule of the Roman church, of course, do not allow divorce under any circumstances whatever."[18] In France divorce was unknown until 1792 but, "In that year the convention went to the other extreme, admitting divorce not only by mutual consent, but even for incompatibility of temper, alleged by one party."[19] Marriage laws in France fluctuated with political changes until 1884 when divorce was granted for the more severe offences. In Germany divorce was formerly granted for ten serious offences but the law was made more stringent in 1900, the number of allowable causes being reduced to five. In the Scandinavian countries, Denmark and Sweden have strict divorce laws, but Norway is mildly liberal, permitting divorce after a separation of three years. Portugal since 1910 has allowed divorce by mutual consent, under certain conditions. Thus the divorce laws of European states present bewildering contrasts. One observes four general types: first, countries in which no divorce is allowed (under the influence of the Roman Catholic Church) ; second, countries under the influence of the Greek Church, run-

[18] *Ibid.*, p. 225.
[19] *Ibid.*, p. 226.

ning back to the Code of Justinian; third, those influenced by the Code Napoleon; fourth, the Protestant countries. In the last three groups the tendency is toward placing men and women on the same basis as regards divorce and the granting of a separation for the more serious offences. England falls into the last group though the situation is really unique.

In the United Kingdom divorce laws are peculiar. In Scotland, for example, the law of 1573, recognizing "desertion" and "adultery" as valid causes, still holds today. In England not until 1857 was divorce allowed, and until 1884, at least in theory, the courts could enforce an order for the restitution of conjugal rights by imprisonment. With one exception the British colonies have moved in the direction of greater liberality. Canada, under the influence of the Roman religion, is the exception; only a few scattered divorce courts have been established there.

Canada's next door neighbor to the south has the most peculiar and complicated divorce situation to be found anywhere. This grows out of the right of each state in the United States to enact its own legislation controlling divorce,—a right fully exercised.

The divorce laws in modern states seem to move in the direction of allowing divorce for behavior that makes married life impossible and unbearable. Such behavior is adultery, cruelty, persistent drunkeness, habitual desertion, and serious crime. There is also a more radical movement which is growing to regard marriage as a contract voidable like other contracts with safe-guards against fraud and against suffering by the children. "In ethics, the change that it (*i.e.*, marriage) has undergone may be expressed by saying that from being a sacrament in the magical, it has become one in the ethical sense."[20] The broad movement of his-

[20] *Ibid.*, p. 231.

tory has been toward a more close-knit family and yet
one which guaranteed equal freedom to both parties.
The problem involved is that of reconciling the claims
of personality and the duties of a common life.

Up to this point consideration has been given to
social evolution as it touches law and justice, marriage
and the position of women. It was necessary also to
make a critical examination of the use made by the
author of ethnological material, and the conclusion was
reached that the comparative and statistical methods
as used raised grave doubts as to the authenticity of
many generalizations reached in this field. Law and justice have advanced slowly along a tortuous path that
moved in the general direction of sanity and human
understanding in both the definition and treatment of
crime. Marriage has moved toward closer union and
greater respect and freedom for the members of the
union. Consideration will now be given to three great
problems of the community: its external relations, class
relations, and the problem of poverty and riches.

4. Inter-Community Relations

Turning, then, from problems of sex to those of
inter-community relations, Hobhouse indicates that
there are also certain broadly definable trends running
through from the dim beginnings of history till modern
times. In the early stages of human history *rights* and
duties belonged to human beings as members of groups,
not as individual personalities. Morality is in its origin
group morality. Today, the groups into which people
are divided carry with them special obligations, but
these need not conflict with the wider obligations of
society. We have group morality where the wider obligation is ignored or put aside in favor of the narrower.
A large section of comparative ethics is devoted to the
transition from group morality to wider ideas of social
obligation.

In primitive society, generally organized on a small group basis, certain disputes arise which bring resort to arms. Fighting over the infringement of border rights is frequent and may be carefully regulated. The number of people to take part in the fight and the implements to be used are established as in dueling. Noncombatants from both sides may mingle freely and with apparent good-will while the fighting is in progress. While there are thus observable in established warfare the germs of moral feeling, of honor, and of fair play, these sometimes tend to make the warfare more vindictive and brutal, one's animus being directed toward individual members of the enemy group. War becomes feud. The conquered has no rights of immunity or protection; he is *rightless* and treated as best suits the convenience of the victor. The unhappy loser may be killed, enslaved, tortured, eaten, adopted, ransomed, exchanged or liberated as chances to suit the victor. Torture, among the simpler peoples, reached it most extreme development among the North American Indians. Cannibalism often has imaginary religious significance yet at times a purely materialistic value. "There comes, indeed, a stage, perhaps the most revolting in the history of human development, at which the weaker tribes are made almost to perform the function of cattle in the economy of life for the stronger."[21] Traces of cannibalism are found in North America, and in ancient Mexico it probably reached its greatest development. Closely connected with cannibalism is head hunting, and a horrible feature of this practice is that oftentimes the head of a woman or child is as much prized as that of a man. However, a time comes in social development when a live prisoner is worth more than a dead one and consequently the loser is enslaved

[21] *Ibid.,* p. 240.

instead of being eaten or used as an outlet for hate. Slavery has flourished more among people capable of steady labor than among hunters or fighters. We may then expect to find war and slavery becoming more closely linked as man gives up nomadic habits.

The early civilizations show an essentially changed picture of warfare. With increased industry to use slaves and bettered techniques for acquiring them the natural desire to exterminate or eat one's fallen enemy was somewhat restrained. Many Egyptian war operations were really slave raids. Yet while war was ruthless the idea of a regular treaty with a foreign people was well understood. As regards cruelty in warfare the Assyrians will probably remain the obvious example of naked boasting over the ferocity of warfare. Assurnasirpal (885 B.C.) records: "To the city of Kinabu I approached . . . I captured it. Six hundred of their fighting men I slew with the sword, three thousand of their captives I burned with fire."[22] He further boasts of large numbers whose hands or feet were cut off, whose nose or ears were struck off, whose eyes were put out. Yet the Assyrian case is not unique in cruelties practiced.

Among the early Hebrews the religious motive carried extermination to the extreme. Fear of contamination caused the issuance of orders for the Canaanite cities to be utterly destroyed; Jericho was to be "devoted" to Jehovah; oftentimes nothing that breathed was to be spared. In the civil wars of early Hebrews indiscriminate massacres were sometimes practiced.

The book of *Deuteronomy*, however, does make certain regulations intended to ameliorate the lot of female captives. Another ethical germ is seen in the case of Joshua, who, having been tricked into an oath with a foreign group, stood by it. With the later Prophets

[22] Quoted, *ibid.*, p. 249.

the conception of universal peace and brotherhood is sometimes glimpsed,—as it had been previously by certain wise men in the east.

Both in Hindu and Chinese ethics war takes a lower place than in Western civilization. In India the priestly class is put above the warrior and Buddhism makes the taking of life under any conditions a crime. The Chinese thinkers deprecate war, which in early times was thoroughly barbaric. The classical books of China set forth the superiority of peaceful to warlike methods. In certain cases these methods come perilously near excusing cowardice. In the teachings of Mencius there is genuine and very strenuous opposition to war and militarism, and he showed great psychological understanding of the "military mind." Lack of imagination for the sufferings of others, he indicated, is one of the forces perpetuating war. His prescription for becoming a universal monarch was not the road of military conquest. The end might be consummated through proving oneself the best and most just of monarchs. Unfortunately not all the world is as peacefully inclined as ancient China.

In the Western world Hobhouse sees a different picture both in ancient Greece and in Rome—republic and empire. In Homeric Greece wars were often waged for women, for cattle, or for other valuables, and it was quite ruthlessly carried forward. However, the Greeks were perhaps the first to develop regular international law. Various forces were at work counteracting the generally accepted war psychology and curtailing the ravages of war. Feuds were replaced by defensive alliances for a limited length of time. A regular system for arbitration was developed and the whole principle of Greek warfare was challenged by the philosophers. Aristotle sets forth that Hellenes should never be made slaves; the "natural" slaves, he held, were those barbarians from outside the peninsula. At Rome, a defeated enemy was in principle rightless; *stranger* and *enemy* are identical terms. The conquered were often put to death in great numbers; even the good emperor Titus killed or sold into slavery all those taken at the capture of Jerusalem. However, public opinion of the Roman world was against such extreme barbarity. War profoundly changed the structure of Roman life; it was the importation of large numbers of slaves that changed the economic system and ultimately contributed to the downfall of the Republic. Yet as Roman conquests extended, more and more of self-government was allowed to the local area and the tributary conquered people in it. The Roman empire when it was overthrown was gradually approaching the ideal of a world state in which distinctions of nationality carry no distinctions of privilege. It is not alone in the realm of political history, however, that one traces out the roots of a changing attitude toward international relations.

Leaving the political states and measuring the influence of the Western religions, Hobhouse finds important currents running both in the Christian and Mohammedan worlds. The *Koran* assumes that peace will exist between believers; no Moslem captive, in theory, can be enslaved. Not so with unbelievers for it is assumed that with them perpetual war exists; the men may be killed without mercy, but the women are to be spared. Christian teachings have effects that are quite complex. While the gospels pronounce against violence in any form, the early fathers condoned war. According to Ambrose non-resistence is unworthy, and generally the Fathers upheld defensive warfare. It follows from their teachings that the lives of non-combatants, as well as of captives, are to be spared. However, during the Middle Ages warfare with horrible barbarities was carried on over Europe. Such a situation inevitably brought protests.

Grotius, in decrying warfare, appealed to the "law of nature," to which nations, in his view, are subject as are individuals. Universal attributes of humanity were relied upon and by going beneath the superficial differences of men—language, custom, dress—he cut the props from under the old group morality. The citizen or the soldier is not personally at fault and cannot be held guilty for the conduct of his government. These principles that Grotius laid down have been both broadened and made more specific through the Convention of Geneva in 1864, and the Hague Conventions of 1899 and 1907. Since this last date the World War and the League of Nations have made their appearance on the stage of history together with a variety of minor characters. Hobhouse points out the great difficulty in establishing international peace. It grows out of the fact that there is no authority, except good-will or the fear of reprisals, to enforce the codes, and that military necessity is used as a cloak to defend the most barbaric practices. "In ethical theory and in the customs which it has codified, the civilized world has sought to safeguard the obligations of humanity and the rights of the person."[28] War is waged against *states* not against *individuals* and the vanquished are not to be deprived of rights which civilized codes accept as inherent in human beings.

A further question, concerning which there is much confusion, remains to be answered: do groups of mankind have rights simply through being groups of human beings? Does a small nation, or minority linguistic group, have any rights even though it has no force to require its rights? This whole question has received

---

[28] *Ibid.*, p. 265.

extraordinary publicity since the World War and probably there is not as much confusion regarding it as formerly. Nevertheless we still find many an individual who swings from callous insistence on material rights to sheer sentimentality. For most people right is right even when (as in international relations) there is no power to enforce the right. Hobhouse stresses the significant fact that the whole war philosophy.has been attacked to some purpose by the Society of Friends. Its protest has set the military spirit the task of justifying itself and that justification is usually "self-defence." Yet history shows the phrase "self-defence" is usually a cloak for aggression.

In England the doctrine of natural liberty, upheld by Cobden and the free traders, tended to discredit the war views of the times and cynical notions of national isolation. Gladstone following Fox, "utterly broke with the doctrine of state morality and rested international dealings on the simple ground of right and wrong as applicable to all other human relations."[24] Mazzini and Comte thought of each nation as a member of a family of nations, making up humanity, and having certain duties and rights in virtue of that position. "Just as international law rests in its beginning on the conception of humanity as incarnate in the person of every human being, so, in the consummated conception of right and brotherhood between nations, it touches the other pole of modern ethics—the conception of humanity as a whole, the sum of all human beings and their collective history. In this conception the old group morality disappears." This is compatible with the view that "the true partriotism is the cornerstone of true internationalism."[25]

[24] *Ibid.*, p. 268.
[25] *Ibid.*, pp. 268-269.

In the view of Hobhouse, international relations show a genuine ethical advance however slow and hesitating it has been. Warfare is directed against a group and no longer with vindictive hatred concentrated upon certain individuals in the enemy group. The conquered are no longer regarded as rightless simply because they are conquered. The war philosophy is not accepted without challenge. Hobhouse believes that a projection of the line of evolution will bring us, sooner or later, to a society of nations, so constituted that each independent nation owes its allegiance to it. But there are other important lines of social evolution to be considered,—notably those relating to classes within the group and to property.

5. Class and Caste

Leaving the external relations of community and following its internal structure and method of functioning, certain long-time trends are pointed out by Hobhouse. The primitive community is usually small, but compact and homogeneous. There are, of course, distinctions between the sexes in their rights, and between the group and the outsider. Morality is confined to the group, and it is out of this fact that class relations grow. Group morality leads on the one side to war and on the other to slavery and serfdom. The *slave* may properly be considered the man whom law and custom regard as the property of another, in extreme cases as a chattel. The *serf* has certain rights, as that of inheriting property, and he cannot easily be dislodged from the land; but he works under the direction of another and is judged and punished by another. Slavery and serfdom are not widespread among the simplest of the primitive people.

The savage enjoys freedom and equality, not because he has realized their value, but, because, due to the structure of society, he is not strong enough to put himself above his neighbor. However, the conception of a certain group of men with limited rights is widely diffused throughout the uncivilized world. Slavery has its special home in Negro Africa, where the groups in which it does not exist are relatively rare. Among the simpler peoples of today, as we pass from the lower hunters to the highest agricultural groups, the percentage of peoples holding slaves rises steadily. And along with this naturally enough the proportion of groups having a definite noble class increases. The slave becomes a real economic asset with settled residence and complex culture techniques. In many slave-holding groups "rightlessness" is qualified. The child of the slave is normally a slave, but in addition in most barbaric and semi-civilized societies slavery is increased by debt, crime, and numerous other causes. Strangely enough the enslaving of debtors has had a softening influence on the institution of slavery, for the family of the debt slave, however illogical it may seem, will not allow unlimited cruelty to be practiced upon one of their own.

It is possible in a thumb nail sketch of the slave systems of great ancient civilizations to observe in process important changes in human class relationships. In the early Babylonian Empire, slaves were chattels. They were branded; oftentimes fettered. If killed, the price of the slave must be paid to his master to compensate for the property loss. Yet later, in the New Kingdom, the slaves often appear transacting important business, so their position was not utterly bad. The ranks of ancient Egyptian slavery were recruited largely from captives and from the slave trade. Subject peoples were required to furnish definite quotas and also tributes of girls. Rameses III, during thirty years, presented to the temples over one hundred and thirteen thousand slaves. Apparently the slaves were entirely at the disposal of the masters. Slavery was not, however, the most important source of labor, for Egypt was thoroughly organized upon a feudal basis. Those who worked on the land were ruthlessly treated by tax collectors and were frequently subjected to forced labor on the king's or a noble's land, or in constructing the pyramids and other public works. Murder of a slave by a serf was punished by death, not out of respect for the slave but because the emperor put slave and serf in the same class.

The laws of slavery among the early Hebrews draw sharp distinctions between Jew and Gentile. According to strict interpretation of the ancient law no Jew should be held permanently as a slave but must be liberated at the end of six years. If, however, the master had provided the slave with a wife, both she and her children remained the property of the master. If the slave preferred wife and children to freedom without them, "then his master shall bring him unto God (that is, to the temple) and shall bring him to the door or unto the doorpost, and his master shall bore his ear through with an awl; and he shall serve him forever."[26] The rule for liberation of slaves in the seventh year was never carried out and later the period was lengthened to fifty, the year of Jubilee being the designated time. The Priestly Code again drew the distinction between Jew and Gentile in the slave relation, and softened some of the rules governing it.

In India slavery was known in the Vedic Age and the institution persisted in the Brahmanic period. According to the code of Manu there were seven kinds of slaves, varying from those captured in war to those held in punishment for crime. A Brahman does not quarrel with his slave; he treats him as his shadow.

[26] Quoted from *Exodus*, XXI, 2-6; *ibid.*, p. 287.

The rules for punishment of slaves were not as severe as those of the Hebrews. However, slavery is of small importance in India compared to caste.

Out of the residence of a light skinned Aryan minority among a dark skinned conquered people came, apparently, the caste institution. "Varna," a Sanskrit word for caste, originally meant color. The Sudra, or lowest caste, was almost rightless and Manu believed that the Sudra was *born* to servitude and could not be freed. He is at the bottom of the social scale, the twice-born ones—priests, warriors, farmers—being above him and having a clear right to exploit him. A Brahman was at liberty to take for his sacrifice any article he needed from a Sudra. To kill a Sudra is of course a minor offence, while if he in turn attempts to teach a Brahman his duty, hot oil is to be poured into his mouth and ears. How could such social organization be justified? The moralists taught that caste grew out of difference in character.

In the teaching of Buddha, on the other hand, there was no thought of caste and "the true Brahman" was he who lived the pure and holy life.

In China a tradition is preserved of a time when there was no slavery, but by the Cho dynasty it was well established. It is a very ancient institution and is general even today. Slave trade in general, even the sale of a daughter by her parents, or of a wife by her husband, especially during famines, is common. Kidnapping also forms a primary source of supply for the slave trade. A master who kills his slave is only punished with the bamboo.

We turn from the Orient to the Near East in sketching the history of class relations. Mohammed found slavery well established, and did what he could to mitigate the lot of the slave, since he could not abolish the institution. Masters are told to be kind to slaves, prostitution of slave girls is a religious offence; masters are encouraged to emancipate a slave whenever he can redeem himself; the freeing of a slave is an act of great religious value, and separating mother and child a grave offence. However, Mohammedan recognition of slave traffic continues, and to this day it is a curse to Africa and a disturbance to world politics.

In the ancient Greece of Homeric times slavery was fully established. Under the recognized formula of warfare when a town was captured the men were killed and the women and children enslaved. Piracy, which was hardly less legitimate than war, was a frequent source of slaves. In the rural districts slavery was rare but with the growth of cities and the increase of wealth the institution became deeply entrenched. The fatal idea that work is undignified for a free man grew naturally with slavery. In Solon's time the land was cultivated for the rich owner and if the poor tenant did not pay five-sixths of his produce to the landlord he fell into serfdom. Solon prohibited debt slavery and this reacted favorably on all forms of serfdom. In a court of law a slave could ordinarily give evidence only under torture and against his master only on a charge of treason. He was allowed, however, to hold property and to have a family. He might purchase his freedom by entrusting his savings to a priest.

An illuminating light on the class relations of the Empire to the west of Greece is reflected by the fact that Rome not only enslaved enemies, but, even down to the time of Justinian, permitted any unprotected foreigner to be enslaved. A free Roman could not become a slave within Rome itself, yet this statement must be taken with caution for it did not apply to selling military deserters abroad, to the selling of children by their parents, debtors by creditors, and the thief by the injured party. In the early period a slave was in law a chattel, but about 19 A.D. a law came into effect forbidding the throwing of slaves to wild beasts without a judicial decision.

Under Antonius Pius the master who killed his slave without cause was punishable as a homicide. Later, the slave cruelly treated could claim the right to be sold to another master and through a special refinement of the law "cruelty" was held to exist if an educated slave was compelled to do manual work. In addition to slavery Rome evolved a system of serfdom on the land. This system, with many modifications, was to form the economic basis of European society for many centuries after the Roman Empire had crumbled.

In the Middle Ages there were two classes of the unfree: slaves proper, and serfs of various types. During the late Empire the doctrine of a common humanity in Stoic philosophy was a moral influence aiding the slaves. This was replaced by the Church doctrine which attempted to minimize an evil it could not cure. Now for the Stoic all men were brothers, there was no distinction of nationality, class, or creed; "For the Church all men ought to be brothers, but many men were, unfortunately, unbelievers, and the brotherhood of men was for many purposes limited to members of the Church."[27] Thus the holding of Christian slaves was deprecated and gradually abolished. However, the Slavs, not for a long time converted, gave slavery a large source of supply. The word "serf" is a modified form of "Slav."

The conversion of the Slavs still left debt slavery and the sale of members of the family by the father as sources of supply, but these, too, gradually disappeared. Slavery depended upon group morality, and the church

[27] *Ibid.*, p. 301.

dealt with it not from the point of view of the rights of the slaves, but of the duties of the master. It took little account of the world outside of the brotherhood of Christ. Thus long afterwards when Negro slavery arose the group morality of the church did not stand out against it but justified it since certain heathen might be converted through slavery. By the end of the twelfth century slavery was almost unknown in Europe; it was being replaced by another servile system,—slavery gave way to serfdom.

The early history of serfdom is obscure. It represents on the one hand progress from slavery, on the other, the degradation of free men. It tended throughout the Middle Ages to lose its domestic character and assume a territorial one. The lot of the serf was gradually ameliorated, and with the rise of the cities his chance of escaping and becoming free increased. Serfdom gradually disappeared in France and England, yet in the middle of the fourteenth century elements of the system persisted in England.

According to Blackstone the laborer stood in the following position: first, the law compelled all persons with no visible effects to work; second, it defined hours of labor; third, it punished those who deserted work; fourth, it empowered justices to fix the rates of wages for agricultural laborers. While these laws were really dead letters they show the spirit of the upper class at that time.

Caste distinctions in England are further shown by the "benefit of clergy," through which (in the middle of the seventeenth century) a man guilty of a small offence went free if he could read. Punishment for petty offences and the preliminary judicial processes for graver crimes were in the hands of the landed gentry. Wages, so fixed as to keep the working classes on the verge of pauperism, were set by the same justices that controlled the poor law, so that any laborer turning there for relief faced essentially the same group. The position of the laborer was worse than under the lighter forms of serfdom. Moreover, the first stages of the factory system made matters worse, for child slavery, in essence, grew up among pauper children. They were brought into the manufacturing district as "apprentices" and worked under terrible conditions. When the public realized this situation laws were passed protecting the children from their legal guardians and bettering conditions of labor. England moved by slow stages while other countries sometimes leaped forward.

On the Continent direct manumission of serfs was more frequent than in England, whole towns on occasion being set free. In 1779 Louis XVI enfranchised the serfs of the royal domain; ten years later, with the Revolution, serfdom was entirely abolished. In Germany after the thirteenth century the conditions of the peasant grew worse until he revolted in the Peasants' War at the time of the Reformation.

Indirectly, the liberation of the German serf came as a result of the French Revolution, for Prussia was preparing to resist France and needed the loyalty of its servile class. The serf was freed by edict in 1807. In the greater part of the Austrian Empire serfdom continued until 1841; it was legally abolished in Russia in 1861. This was the last chapter in the enslavement of the white man.

One observes here parenthetically that no mention has been made of the widespread peonage in Central and South America. The peon, however, is usually an Indian or mixed-breed and might not be classed as "white." "The later stages of the process in the more backward countries were thus clearly deliberate acts of the government, based upon general conceptions either of humañ rights or of the conditions of social wellbeing."[28]

In one way the abolition of slavery and serfdom was an advance from a smaller to a larger group morality, —allowing certain elemental moral principles to apply to all white Christians. Yet morality remained in essence something to be used *in one's group*, however large that group might be, and this was shown when a test came. The Portuguese began importing Negro slaves in 1442 and Pope Nicholas V in 1454 sanctioned it on the ground that the Negroes might be converted to the Christian faith. The hope of saving souls paralyzed the protest of humanitarians against a reversion to one of the worst features of barbarism. Columbus, following the custom of the time, shipped five hundred Indians to Spain but Isabella had them returned to their home. Las Casas observed the high death rate among Indian slaves and so, with all good intention, suggested the use of Negro slaves in the New World. The slave business grew apace and all the great trade nations of Europe entered into the business of transporting the Negroes. From the sixteenth to the eighteenth centuries even the popes had galley slaves,—in this case Turkish. Negro slavery, however, was not destined to last as long as the preceding white slavery.

This second wave of slavery was checked by a distinctly ethical movement beginning with the Quakers in the seventeenth century. Slavery was abolished in Great Britain early in the nineteenth century and later in the century in France, Portugal, Holland, the United States, and Brazil,—in the last named country in 1888.

Obviously the problem of dealing with colored labor has not been solved though real progress has been made. The modern tendency toward great concentration of

[28] *Ibid.,* p. 311.

wealth combined with vast reserves of cheap labor in China and Africa reproduce in essential features the very conditions out of which great slave systems of the past arose. Statesmen cannot neglect the possibilities of using this cheap, docile labor of the East against organized labor in the West.

This historic sketch of class relations shows the group morality of a class in society gradually expanding to include a larger number of individuals and slowly softening its stern outlines as one obligation after another is recognized as having universal application. Hobhouse believes we shall move forward in the direction of a universalism where class distinctions will play an insignificant role. Attention is next directed to the history of poverty and riches, the final section in the sketch of the broad lines of social evolution.

6. Poverty and Riches

"Speaking very roughly, we may say that humanity has hitherto known three stages of economic development. In the first, the fruits of the earth are open to all to gather. There is general poverty, but also general opportunity. In the second, labor, like all social life, is more organized, men have their status of master or slave, lord or vassal, superior or dependent. There is discipline but not freedom. In the third, while the individual is free to make his own career within the limits of the social order, it falls out, through the working of competition and the cumulative factor of inheritance, that there are those who have a lien on the fruits of earth in the industry of others, and those—and they are the majority—who have none. The man of property and the man of none are the contrasted figures of modern civilization, and their reconciliation a problem which becomes more urgent as industrialism advances."[29]

Among primitive peoples, according to Hobhouse, there is little scope for the institution of private property apart from a bit of land and small personal belongings. These properties are held on the principle of occupation and use. Where social organization is simple, property rights are on the same footing as other rights. The most important social question about property rights relates to "ownership of the means of production." Access to the land, for the able bodied, means maintenance, and the significant evolution of property in early phases is that concerning land ownership.

Among the hunting peoples as a whole the authorities most frequently deny individual or family ownership of land, though it is often held in common by a section of a tribe, clan, or local group. Tribal or clan ownership is subject to certain regulations tending to equalize the chances of obtaining food and of preventing starvation. Sometimes custom requires the hunter to take the smallest or worst portion of the kill. Exact and minute division of the spoil is often set forth. When agriculture begins it is generally in a clearing of which the fertility is soon worked out; a new clearing is made and the process repeated. Consequently ownership of land can hardly exist.

As tillage develops, land of value tends to become a permanent possession. Thus private ownership grows out of occupation. Much land also falls into the hand of the chief, and his power varies from nominal control to despot. As his power grows there comes, naturally enough, the rise of aristocracy to support that power and profit by it. With all this comes the landless tenant cultivator. Among the simpler peoples of today the proportion of groups holding property com-

[29] *Ibid.*, p. 332.

munally decreases from the lower hunters to the higher agriculturalists. However, there is no corresponding rise in individual ownership though there is increased ownership by chief and nobles. These last two statements are based on the comparative study of ethnological material by Hobhouse. The communism of the early village gradually wastes away though a smaller scale communism of the joint family continues. However, within this small group forms of private property are seen. For example, a daughter's property remains hers after marriage. Private property produces a basis for the free exchange of goods, beginning apparently in gift swapping, and there develops naturally commerce, division of labor, and free industrial enterprise. Once it is recognized, the contract as an element in social life constantly increases in importance, consequently it has become progressively easier for social resources to be used wherever they bring the largest return. Today capital passes state frontiers with ease. Yet free contract and private property bring many acute social problems, and few countries leave industrial contracts entirely unregulated, recognizing an element of injustice in such a procedure.

As property and trade increase some grow rich, others poor, and this raises the question of the treatment of those members of society in dire distress. This in turn brings up the ethical question of society's attitude toward the helpless. Among primitive peoples a bright side of their life is the liberality of giving both directly to those in need and through hospitality. Primitive man may abandon the helpless or put them to death, such action being regarded as necessary among some nomads and fully sanctioned by custom, yet he willingly shares food and shelter with the unfortunates that remain.

In the earlier civilizations family solidarity, perhaps with ancestor worship added, secured good treatment for the old and infirm. In ancient Egypt kind treatment for the poor and the aged was regarded as a virtue; the Babylonian writings indicate that failure in duty to the helpless is a great sin; in China respect for the aged is a cornerstone of ethics along with the duty of filial obediance; in India almsgiving was recognized as a meritorious act, but in fullness goes to caste-fellows alone. Hebrew legislation attempted to prevent usury in the interests of the poor. The law of Islam upholds almsgiving, and usury is forbidden; the spoils of the enemy were to be used for the poor. Later the Mohammedans established a poor tax of about one fortieth of all that had been in the believer's possession during the year. At one time a pension plan was established. In all these early societies there was at least the recognition of an obligation to unfortunates however imperfectly it may have been fulfilled.

During the classical period of Greece citizens of Crete and Sparta, rich and poor alike, were maintained at the public table. In Athens down to Solon's time the property of a childless person reverted to the clan and was used to support all orphans. Hippocrates laid down the rule that a doctor's first duty on entering a town was to attend to the sick poor. In Rome, the tendency toward centralization in the capital tended to push the poor further and further down the economic scale. To combat this, legislation provided for the distribution of corn to Roman citizens at half price; later the corn was made free and portions of oil, wine, and clothing were probably added to it. This custom spread to Alexandria, Antioch, and Constantinople and fostered a vast, idle city population.

In the first century A.D., hospitals with infirmaries for sick slaves were established in Rome with a physician for the poor in attendance. Most of the poor at this period belonged to funeral benefit societies. The Emperor Trajan lent money at low interest to municipalities to care for destitute children. Within the vast Roman state a variety of methods were used in caring for the needy.

With the break-up of the empire the burden of poor relief fell upon the church. During Charlemagne's time the tithe became legal, and out of it the priests were instructed to support the poor. Moreover almsgiving was virtuous, and voluntary poverty was set up as an ideal. Later, Protestantism gave impulse to a movement to substitute public relief of the poor for ecclesiastical relief. The destitute received better care until with the sixteenth century there came two set-backs: the suppression of monasteries and the enclosure of arable land for pastures. One cut off a source of relief and the other restricted the labor market, between them bringing a great increase of pauperism.

Severe legislation against wandering beggars was a favored method of dealing with poverty. Edward VI offered the beggars as temporary slaves to the first comer. However, England reacted against this barbarity, and by the act of 1601 it acknowledged the obligation of society to relieve its poor members from destitution. Overseers with power to levy taxes to support the indigent were appointed. But England was not yet out of the woods, for this system led to many inequalities and threatened working people with a new serfdom through an Act of Settlement in 1662 which forbade them to move about seeking employment. Moreover it brought pauperization in those districts where the law was laxly administered. The Poor Law of England was revolutionized in 1834 and many important changes have taken place since that day.

Most governments today acknowledge their obligation to prevent actual starvation, yet there is a vital distinction to be drawn between poverty and pauperism. Poverty is a social disease and effort directed to discovering causes and remedies is the rational approach. Little has been done in this direction, yet it is something to have reached the point where general agreement exists that poverty is neither a blessing nor a necessity.

The history of poverty and riches in human society presents an interesting evolution to the mind of Hobhouse. Early man is so completely a part of his group that the sphere of private property is small. There is little wealth and few cases of poverty except that poverty shared on occasion by all. Land belongs to the group; power of private contract is small. Later a few individuals have privileges, but for the great bulk of the population caste distinctions and feudal relations make one thing certain: a man is born, lives, and dies in precisely the same station in society. Not until crippling distinctions before the law have been abolished is it possible for the child born to black bread and beer to dine in old age upon caviar and champagne. The crippling distinctions were not abolished until comparatively recent times and many are the tales of beggar boys turned millionaire. But if a few have grown very rich many more have grown very poor. Faced with this situation society has tried every form of stupid treatment of poverty—from blind and pauperizing charity to blind and useless cruelty. Only now is the notion beginning to get abroad that poverty, a social disease, may be treated with as much detachment as measles.

This concludes the brief review of the Hobhousian scheme of social evolution. In the phases considered,— law and justice, women and marriage, war and inter-community relations, class and caste, property and

poverty—important historic trends toward a better solution of each problem have been indicated. One of the
interesting things about the social theory of this writer
is the way all the segments fit together; there are no
jarring contraditions, every part meshes with every
other. This will become increasingly evident as the various aspects of his social theory are considered.

IV. THE PSYCHOLOGICAL-PHILOSOPHICAL
BASIS OF SOCIAL THEORY

The sociological "System" of Hobhouse, set forth in summary form in. his four most recent volumes,[1] is called by him "a synthesis of the philosophic and scientific methods of social inquiry."[2] With this warning one is prepared for a complicated admixture of philosophic theory and social theory; moreover, if one has read conscientiously the previous writings of Hobhouse, it will not be surprising to find most critical points settled by reference not to specific facts but to broad philosophic principles.

It follows under such a method of procedure that one must be very sure of one's broad philosophic principles. Naturally then Hobhouse sets these forth in considerable detail; he gives their history from earliest times, criticizes contrary views, and fills many closely reasoned pages with a defense of his own positions. This may account for a neglect of Hobhouse in America almost as complete as though his writings were in the Russian language. Yet the curse lying upon philosophy is in this case a double curse, resting also upon the one who observes it, for one finds in these writings many important considerations entirely apart from philosophy.

Since the present study is concerned primarily with sociology the philosophic sections will be clipped to the minimum consistent with a coherent review of his system.

[1] *The Metaphysical Theory of the State; The Rational Good; The Elements of Social Justice; Social Development.*

[2] *Social Development* opposite title page.

Fundamental to social theory is a scheme of *ends* or values to the individual which are to fit him into his social group and the wider society. Hobhouse has considered this question in detail and posited a rational good as the basis of his social theory.[3] How this rational good has developed, what part reason plays in practical life, whether human conduct so closely bound up with emotion and impulse can be dominated by such intellectualistic conceptions, are questions considered. In another place the attempt is made to fit the abstract principles here set forth to the major social problems of a complex industrial civilization. In the present critical review the method of deriving the abstract principles is gone over briefly in order that greater attention may be given in the next chapter to the treatment of present problems; the philosophy is touched lightly, the sociology stressed. Attention is now turned to his psychological-philosophical position.

It is generally conceded, Hobhouse holds, that emotion dominates human action and the effective rules of conduct are rather those formulating what man feels than those telling him what he ought to feel. Much of psychological analysis sees in the alleged "reasons" for action an expression of underlying impulses. Man first wishes to do something and then goes about the process of finding suitable reasons for carrying out his wishes; a man loves a woman not because she is beautiful but she is beautiful because he loves her. In the Bank Islands it is customary to place a piece of banana trunk on the bosom of a dead mother. This is said to fool the ghost so that it will not destroy the baby. In reality the Bank Islander does not wish to deprive the mother of her infant and neither does he wish to destroy the child; between these two wishes he works out a

[3] *Morals in Evolution*, pp. 563-639, and *The Rational Good*, pp. xxii, 237.

compromise. And yet, we are told, how blind is impulse without intellect! Impulse is an explosive power but requires intellect as a directing agent. Witness the manner in which both impulse and intellect function in a legal system.

While it is very easy from historic examples to point to the futility of certain theories in influencing conduct it is usually admitted that other theories do at least have a harmful effect. Thus the notion of Natural Rights held by Rousseau is generally conceded to have led to some of the excesses of the French Revolution. May not theories under other conditions have beneficial effects? Theories arise out of the intellectual situation and must in the end run the gamut of evidential proof however popular they may be in themselves. If they are unsound,—like the theory that the earth is flat—they will eventually disappear, though they die a hard death.

In the preceding paragraphs the great emphasis placed upon reason as the important factor in shaping conduct is typical of Hobhousian theory. Some readers will feel that this involves a misplaced emphasis. The present writer holds that man is rational, if ever, only during those rare moments when he sees in magnificent perspective all the ramifications of one small sector of reality with which he has long been familiar. The economist may see all the implications of a high tariff policy. Can we expect that he will be equally rational in his religious beliefs or in his choice of a wife? The question hardly merits an answer. Recent studies of motivation, both along psychoanalytic lines and from the viewpoint of behaviorists, add new weight to the emphasis upon emotion as opposed to reason. Hobhouse attempts to buttress his position by indicating that emotion is not opposed to reason but is an integral part of it, as he conceives reason.

Now impulse and feeling, and desire which logically follows them, are carefully distinguished by Hobhouse. The essential difference is seen when extreme emotion paralyzes impulse, or when swift and effective impulse seems to satisfy emotion before it is running at full tide. From the evolutionary point of view it is clear that both impulse and feeling along with gross physical modifications conform to physical laws connected with utility in survival. Feeling has the function of guiding impulse and fitting it to meet the conditions of life.

In man the development of the organism makes for the greatest mastering of the conditions of life and there is very wide range within which pleasurable sensations having no survival value may take place. Nevertheless it is survival value, we are told, that governs the formation of the primitive strata of impulse and feeling. Both are altruistic or social in origin to the extent that they have been concerned with others,—with mate, offspring, and other members of the flock or herd. *Feeling* has its psychical side manifesting itself in movements. When an impulse is directed toward an anticipated end, action is truly purposive. Mr. Hobhouse would make a fundamental distinction between this *purposive* action and the simple process of conditioning. At this point *desire* enters the picture, with its roots in impulse and feeling. Following desire we have volition, "a permeating tendency among a body of impulses and desires, or . . . direction of effort toward some comprehensive end, to which a mass of impulses and desires are subordinated as being that which makes their real meaning and value explicit."[4]

Thus step by step is a logical psychology put down to act as a basis for a rational philosophy. Detailed criticism of each point raised would be tedious. In another

[4] *Rational Good,* pp. 45-46.

place exception is taken to much of the material here presented.

When an impulse to an end dominating all life exists, we have will. The function of will is to bring unity to our volition, as the function of volition is to unify desires. Human conduct differs from animal in that a general principle of action tends to correlate behavior; the animal evidently cannot conceive of itself as a persistent identity. Will rests on feeling in the generic sense. Sheer impulse would carry the individual hither and yon; fully developed will would direct all impulse and feeling toward a previously determined end. In the individual personality primary impulses remain and the end of life, toward which will is striving, is not always felt with requisite intensity, so that we have a tug of war between impulse and will.

There is, then, according to the scheme just set forth a clear relation between impulse, feeling, desire, volition, and will. Out of the matrix of these, formed fundamentally of impulse-feeling, comes purposive conduct with certain fundamental drives that push throughout life toward goals held to be important. Out of such an analysis Hobhouse sees the possibility of truly rational behavior emerging. If it does emerge then a rational good may be set up and from it certain implications and applications suggest themselves,—first abstractly and then in relation to present world problems.

When may conduct be termed "rational"? Hobhouse replies in great detail. It is easiest to come at the rational through deciding what is irrational. Now a person's judgments are clearly irrational if they are self-contradictory and inconsistent, if they are arbitrary and groundless, or if based purely on emotion or desire. The rational deals with the objective order, arrived at through exposure of inconsistencies. Truth is the object of the rational procedure and interconnection of different ideas mutually consistent is its method of advance. We must give provisional value to certain judgments, as of sensation, which become established judgments when confirmed by others of a provisional nature. Even general "truths" cannot be accepted as self-evident unless consistent with other observed facts. Obviously a system of thought containing all experience could have no ground of truth outside itself. So long as experience is partial mutual consistency is the only safe ground. "So far as we reason about a thing we treat it as having a ground which connects it with other things, and as this connection can be constantly extended by repetition of the process we arrive at the ideal of reason as an order of reality built up of a system of universals interconnecting all its parts."[5] Reason then is not a faculty to be possessed but a principle to be used in the analysis of reality,—the principle of interconnection persistently applied. The *rational* is thus a process rather than an established system. Does it follow that what is *rational* is also good?

The judgment, "this is good," expresses a disposition and asserts a fact; by the mere expression *good* the individual signifies something which disposes to action. The good for me harmonizes with my disposition and this turns on feeling. A baby tries to grasp a candle flame and effort is broken off, there is disharmony between effort and its end. Pain is felt and disharmony exists. When a child after much reaching gets a sugar plum there is harmony between effort and result, a pleasant feeling tone culminates in satisfaction. Harmony is thus a form of mutual support and interplay between desire and result.

It may be pointed out here that while psychologists of the behaviorist school would explain all this in

[5] *Rational Good.* p. 72.

terms of simple conditioning, Mr. Hobhouse has given a highly intellectualistic explanation of the process, set forth in a different terminology. There is no conflict here as to what happens to the child's behavior patterns once he gets the delectable sugar plum: he will at the next opportunity repeat his previous behavior and try for another one. The fundamental difference is in the amount of conscious intelligence to be assigned the child in this process. The behaviorist "plays down" conscious intelligence often to the vanishing point and Hobhouse most emphatically plays it up. In either case what is *good* is what we *want;* for Hobhouse this is the pleasurable, corrected by the mature judgment of the will. And the will rests in last analysis upon feeling. The fundamental fallacy ordinarily made when one asserts "this is good" is that an expression of attitude is confused with an assertion of fact.

Intellect and reason are often belittled in connection with conduct, Hobhouse holds, because of a misunderstanding of what reason is. It is not to be conceived apart from emotion and experience. Viewed as a whole a person's life is full of inconsistencies, yet while pursuing any given object the person is fairly logical and consistent. This beginning of reason, found in everyone, is the basis of its completer development in truly rational conduct. This relation of reason and emotion is clearly seen in the history of any important social institution; what has taken place in its development reveals that it has not been planned with a far-off goal in view but each step has been taken because certain immediate exigencies had to be met. Intellect, impulse, and feeling all had their part in its growth.

The rational good, then, must be *consistent throughout* and its basis must be objective. It does not rest upon a suppression of natural desires. Whose feelings and desires are to be harmonized in the rational good?

Eventually, everyone's; all the conflicts are to be ironed out. Rational impulse, it would seem, has the function in practice of embracing the world of impulse-feeling in a single system of purposes, just as the rational in cognition attempts to embrace the world of experience in a single system of thought. This involves a harmony of the mind with itself and of mind with others about it. While complete harmony must remain an ideal, it is the function of the rational principle to work persistently toward that ideal. But why not allow an individual to build his own internal harmony out of pure egoism? Because, in the opinion of Hobhouse, one such system would clash with another like it and this would involve two rational systems being inconsistent with each other which *by definition* is impossible. Yet suppose we have a tight little community thoroughly content with its own code, calling everyone in the world outside a barbarian, how can universalism have any force there? In the first place the moral rule holds, just as does the rule of prudence, whether the individual observes it or not. Moral obligation is present even though it is ignored. A man unaware of it is like a blind man choosing colors. However, "The moral impulses are not created by exposition but must be there before we can appeal to them. In the normal man, however, such promptings exist, and assert themselves with varying degrees of actual force against rebellious impulse."[6] All of which will seem rather intellectualistic to some readers. A logical analysis of philosophic concepts seems to reduce human nature to an abstraction.

The main elements of impulse-feeling evolve under the conditions of existence in the evolutionary process. Through natural selection types of activity are estab-

[6] *Ibid.,* p. 112.

lished. We are told: "The parental instincts, in fact the sex instinct, and where it exists, the herd instinct, are all impulses of this class."[7] Moreover, "the feelings that bind us to others and overleap the boundary of self are just as primary psychologically as those which interest us in our own future. They are rational in the sense that they are integral parts of a rational synthesis, not in the sense that they are results reached by a deductive reasoning, or by any other purely intellectual process."[8] The unfortunate leaning upon an instinct psychology by Hobhouse has already been referred to elsewhere. His following of McDougall in this is one of his most serious handicaps in the psychological field, it is held by those who cannot agree that the primary springs of human behavior lie in a dozen or so great, all-powerful instincts. It follows from the positions taken that with experience unlimited there is no end to the work of reason; the harmonizing principle may be carried forward indefinitely. There must be the attempt to resolve conflicts in the world of feeling and the environment must be modified to make such transition possible.

Yet how is harmony in the world of feeling to be obtained when every individual has impulses trying to drive him in opposite directions? Must not one or the other impulse be thwarted, thus giving pain? Certainly no good can come from the suppressing of any deep laid impulse but the channel of its outlet may be modified and this is easier if the personality has certain well-marked ends to which all others are merely intermediary. One may begin by inquiring just what the "root interests" of man really are since upon a definition of these hangs any subsequent social theory.

[7] *Ibid.*, p. 119.
[8] *Ibid.*, p. 120.

The roots interests of man cluster about two opposite poles, the selfish and the social. "The social compromise is the reflection of an interpenetrating duality into which the soul of man has grown in adapting itself to the conditions of its existence through the geological period."[9] Its two elements are self assertion and self devotion; selfishness and love. In point of time, maternal love appears as the earliest form of altruism and is deepest laid in original human nature. The evolution of instinct always proceeds from the general to the particular, from the undefined to the defined. Hobhouse states: "I take mother love, parental love and family affection to be not the source but the prime examples of an impulse inherent in mind, and potentially as wide as the range of life, even, we may say, as the universe in its scope."[10] Religion and sex are really branches of one tree; sex love admitting of astonishing ranges from the animal to the spiritual. The youth who loves and finds all the world fair and wishes to do great deeds has a momentary vision of the real meaning of life. The prosaic world, flattening down his enthusiasm, is in error, not the youth. Sex feeling and the closely related religious attitude is a way the individual feels his relation to the universe. This feeling of relation to the whole may come directly, as in patriotism, or indirectly by emotions that link one person to another who in turn is linked to a third, and so on indefinitely in a long chain of emotions uniting the members of a community.

One may pause to inquire whether this grouping of human motives about the two poles of the selfish and the social does not involve an over-simplification of a highly complex situation. Many dichotomies of man's conduct and of the world he lives in have been sug-

[9] *Social Development*, p. 149.
[10] *Ibid.*, p. 151.

gested. One of the most ancient divides man's deeds
between righteous and sinful and his world correspondingly between a benign deity and a malign satan. Some
modern writers asure us that we fluctuate between the
desire for self-preservation and race preservation. Other
dichotomies of human motivation have been suggested
in bewildering number. They have notably one common
weakness when applied to actual behavior situations.
They encounter border line cases that refuse to fall
under either category. Only to the charcoal artist is the
world divided into black and white.

We proceed with the Hobhousian analysis of motives. Affection and sympathy are not the same, a
parent's affection for its child may be both selfish and
domineering. Another closely related root interest is
sympathy—the propensity to do for others as we would
be done by. Sympathy is fundamental to social theory
because it may be heightened by affection, by coöperation, and by mutual understanding. Imagination facili-
tates all of these, consequently imagination is the most
important variable in human intercourse. For fundamentally the social impulse is an impulse to reciprocity;
what we want in others is that when we pipe to them
they shall dance. The self, as Hobhouse conceives it, is
not a separate object but a distinct element in our objects generally; it is that element among our objects
which starts and comes back to the stream of our own
feeling. A backing of self feeling is a healthy element
in life and a measure of pride is necessary; to break
its last element, self respect, is ruin. Self-regard must
be distinguished from the more elementary self asser-
tiveness. There is no necessary conflict between social
feeling and self assertion; the true conflict is between
partial or exclusive interests and comprehensive and
rational ones. Parental feeling is not selfish though it

may be recklessly anti-social, as may religious enthusiasm and patriotism.

Are anti-social feelings after all fundamentally necessary to the human mind? Hobhouse answers with a qualified "no." He holds that antipathy gives rise to ill-will but is not the same thing. Antipathies do seem natural consequences of limited personalities lacking a sense of humor. Antagonism plays a larger part in the background of human nature than we like to allow. Observe the sub-malicious gossip so common in society. As Mr. Dooley says, "What's one man's news is another man's misfortunes." In this we are measuring ourselves by our fellows, and our self-respect is impaired if we fall below them. Hobbes should not have maintained that gratitude is a lively expectation of favors to come; it is rather a firm resolution to be even with our benefactor and so find means of forgiving him. The whole thing regarding anti-social feelings is that the repressions of life, particularly of sex, vent themselves in lashing the unfortunate offender. Strangely enough the denunciation by society of the transgressor of sex *mores* is in part sincere, in that it is a denunciation of similar desires in the denouncers. Note the ever present interest in the sex weakness of others. It would appear then that the back-ground of ill-will is not a primary thing, like sympathy, but a secondary consequence of an exclusive egoism.

Two other root interests are added by Hobhouse,—a constructive and a cognitive. Regarding the latter we observe that a puppy is exceedingly inquisitive though it is a passing phase satisfied after an object has been tested by each of its senses. The child's interest, in contrast with that of the puppy, goes on from a sensory examination of an object to the *why* and *whence* of things. It is an unevenly distributed impulse and more readily atrophied than others. The constructive impulse, as a general interest, is more nearly confined to man. It is visible from the moment the baby begins to pat sand into shape, and persists as a hobby even under discouraging circumstances. Its tendency to outstrip and disregard utility testifies to its independent origin.

If we assume these root interests established how can a many-sided and harmonious self be realized? First of all it must have a system of ends which are mutually consistent and (though every passing impulse must be subordinated to that end) no ineradicable impulse must be left frustrated. The actual life and institutions of any society contain some fragments of rationality asserting itself amid the clash of impulses, and by the extent of these fragments we measure its value.

Harmony in the individual is possible in so far as radical impulses admit of mutual adjustment in their outlets. However, building up a rational order proceeds bit by bit; having reached the stage where the individual has an organized group of impulses to which he gives outlet, he judges good everything that fits into his system. Moreover, the harmony reached through development is more complex and difficult to attain than harmony based on repression. Through the development of personality, with its progressive fulfillment, comes whatever of cohesion and individuality the active man's life manifests, and by it some impress can be made upon the outer world.

The outer world, however, is never entirely external and foreign to the personality; individuality is in large measure a social product. Altruism arises, we are assured, before the distinction of self and others has taken place and it is as irrational to follow a single impulse as to think of the self without reference to the wider group. Yet the normally harmonious outlet for individual impulses must be changed only so far as required by the necessity for harmony with the efforts of others. This leads to a constantly widening circle and ideally would include all humanity; practically, it operates on the principle that each action is to be fitted into the entire scheme of conduct. The body of definite knowledge grows by a kind of mechanical accretion as does the material capital of society,—its roads, buildings, laboratories—but the situation is different in ethical ideas and practice. Here each individual must himself enter through experience into principles already established. Ethical progress is therefore less direct than mechanical advance, though there has been a forward movement. As isolated impulses grow into the *self* or *person,* separate individuals are bound into a *social unity,* and these two movements cover the distance from isolated impulse to complete harmony of activity and feeling. They are based, Hobhouse indicates, on the principles of personality and love. It hardly seems necessary to examine this last concept in detail at this point. Some notes in disagreement have been indicated elsewhere.

So far development has been thought of as a means toward harmony as an end. Yet harmony is also means as well as end. Development at any point is the summing up of the experience that has been brought into a harmonious system. The good is happiness in fulfillment of vital capacity in a world adapted to mind. As indicated, this must ultimately include all mind. All of which is very abstract. How are these abstractions to be applied to the recognized social order that admittedly has many irrational elements?

In last analysis the moral code that underlies social behavior is built on simple direct qualities and its application in broad outline is clear. Perhaps, we are told, these qualities reduce to a combination of courage and tenderness and if these are present in the pure state there exists potentially the whole scheme of a rational life. Yet, how would the principle of harmony aid us in finding our way through the maze of the present moral order and in rebuilding it on more rational grounds. There are, of course, certain general problems of method to be faced. Wherever incompatibility is found in the desires and claims of different groups some modification is necessary but only to the point where conflict disappears. Of course, "all toleration of differences sets a problem to the social intelligence but it is the only problem worth its solving,"—since all difference is potential antagonism.[11] This helps to understand the relation between the principle of harmony and the contention that highest development comes through strife.

There is a deep seated impulse to match one self or one country against another yet it is the rules of the competition which determine whether the antagonism is socially desirable. What most people wish to do is to pass a record established by another. "It is the standard rather than the individual that we want to beat. Competition is thus an imperfect incarnation of the enthusiasm for progress."[12]

After all, however, Hobhouse asks, are all forms of life at bottom capable of harmony? The first answer is that the principle of harmony should be carried as far as possible and the constant attempt made to carry it farther. Refractory impulses that refuse to fit into the scheme rationally set up must be dealt with as the exceptions and obscurities to scientific knowledge are handled. It may be that at a given stage of development two systems will present themselves as equally rational; more likely, however, the one system will be worked out by rationalists while the other has behind it the weight of tradition and authority. The second answer to our

[11] *Rational Good,* p. 179.
[12] *Ibid.,* p. 180.

question is that we may find our way out of the dilemma if we have basic principles of a rational order to which we can tie. There are, it is indicated, three principles of procedure to be followed: (a) "What is good for us must 'work,' if not literally here and now, at least in such continuity with what is here and now that we can fit ourselves into it without any destruction."[13] (b) No restraint is to be imposed not proven necessary to the functioning of the social structure. This is a principle of philosophic liberalism. (c) What is good for A is also good for B unless essential differences between the two can be shown. Thus nationality is the same in central Europe and in Ireland, unless clearly shown to be different. This is a principle underlying philosophic socialism. In applying these principles one must avoid on the one hand the fanaticism of absolute rights, which are non-existent, and on the other hand a worship of institutions as embodiments of the wisdom of the race. The social structure has value only as it serves the individual.

Such then is the scheme of rational good set down by Hobhouse. It is clearly an integral part of his philosophic evolutionary theory and is supported by his view of the history of social institutions, and the importance of mind in the evolutionary process. He gives his position succinctly in a sentence. "The rational harmony contemplated here means neither more nor less than the more perfect adjustment and co-ordination of the permanent forces that make for betterment in the movement in the world, and which, slowly gathering vitality as civilization advances, now mainly require a fuller and more adequate expression to secure to them the ultimate control of the movement of social life."[14]

[13] *Ibid.*, p. 187.
[14] *Ibid.*, p. 234.

One cannot read through the writings of Hobhouse in the field of social ethics without being aware of the intellectual keenness and energy of the man as well as the strength of his convictions. In general the writer believes he has placed more weight on man's feeble intellectual qualities than they can carry. His psychology also seems to be at fault in its reliance upon the instincts, and in an over-simplification of human motivation with its two poles of the selfish and the social. At times his language is strangely reminiscent of a mediaeval metaphysical discourse. We have a principle of love to guide us and a world effort underlying reality and doing its best to bring about a universal harmony. These things cannot detract from the fundamental con-tribution of Hobhouse to social ethics.

Yet in this workaday world how is one to apply the Hobhousian scheme of an evolving rational harmony? What is its relation to ordinary duties and to the nettle-some question of nationality and imperialism? One would inquire of its bearing on social and political freedom, on justice and equality. What of the payment for services? of property and the economic organization? of industrial organization? of democracy? To a consideration of these questions we now turn.

V. SOCIAL THEORY AND PRESENT WORLD PROBLEMS

In seeking a solution of present world problems, Hobhouse, as we have seen, places primary emphasis upon the principle of social and individual harmony. This principle of harmony may fall into the error of one-sided collectivism or one-sided individualism. Hobhouse indicates this clearly. On the one side it is evident that social achievements by their very magnitude sometimes dwarf the individual. Thus the developments of the machine age often crush personality. Yet when proper attention is paid to the human element in production the new powers available will lighten the life of the worker as they have already those of the owner. On the other hand an exaggerated individualism often arises. The successful man boasts of the business which "I" have created. Here the individual claims certain rights as an individual which really belong to him only as a member of society. A right is always one term of an obligation. If a man has an exclusive right to property others have the duty to leave it alone; rights are not outside of social welfare but a part of it. Rights and duties can only be put above the general well-being by denying that the real aim of man is the general well-being.

The individual, then, stands in a double relation to the community: he has a share in it, that is, his *rights;* he must make his contribution,—his *duties.* "A man's right, speaking generally, is a claim upon others which he may make or which may be made for him, and which is maintained by some impartial standard."[1] The theory

[1] *Elements of Social Justice,* p. 36.

of rights applies also to families, communities, and
nationalities. Acknowledged rights take for granted a
community where behavior is organized toward the
common good, and yet acknowledged rights may conflict. What will work out best here and now is often
the only test applied. This expediency "ignores the important truths that the permanent welfare of humanity
rests on definite conditions, that people cannot live from
hand to mouth, but need security and certainty in their
mutual relations as the basis of any fruitful co-opera-
tion."[2] Violation of critically tested "right" is not to
be tolerated.

In politics the most difficult problems for the
statesman come up where two conflicting claims, each
based on substantial grounds, arise. Thus as regards
nationality a difficult situation exists where a small
minority in a certain area is bitterly opposed to the
majority in that area. Their wish for a separate nation
may cut across the claims of another country to an
important port. In this situation there are no absolute
rights of nationality. Yet if the common feeling is very
close-knit the suppression of the desire for nationality
will inevitably involve many other rights being sup-
pressed, such as those of freedom of speech.

Akin to the problem of nationality is that of colonial
expansion or imperialism. Many specious claims are put
forward for advancing the boundaries of empire—the
white man's burden, manifest destiny, etc.; so far as
concerns Great Britain they are all hypocritical. Territory has been added by naked force and border wars are
continuous. The Boer War, fought as a miners' war
to give outlet to surplus English labor, resulted in the
capitalists' importing Chinese labor because they feared
the labor party. Suppression and not freedom has followed the advance of the army; in some areas where the

[2] *Ibid.,* p. 40.

worker is "stimulated" a condition approaching slavery exists. In England the absorption of attention in foreign affairs has paralyzed the democratic effort at home. Thus imperialism began with the violation of a few rights but inevitably progressed to an over-riding of many others.[3]

Much of imperialist policy has been based upon a belief in racial superiority, and the whole of the Hobhousian social theory is attacked by many writers who approach the problem of human welfare from a narrowly biological point of view. To the extreme eugenists, Hobhouse pays his compliments. He is careful in doing this to indicate his adherence to a moderate eugenic program based upon a sound and duly modest biology and in line with a broadly humanitarian social philosophy. Those strands of heredity which are unquestionably bad, he would eliminate. Society must assure itself that the stock is so bad that its elimination would bring a net gain. Whenever clear evidence is brought forward of the hereditary nature of insanity or feeble-mindedness or alcoholism or syphilis, society should prevent such stock from perpetuating itself. However any attempt to identify biological unfitness with poverty or pauperism is not to be tolerated.

That poverty as such is offered as proof of biological unfitness is clear evidence to Hobhouse that many writers on eugenics lack the most elementary knowledge of the social process. "One would suppose it axiomatic that without perfect equality of opportunity actual position in the social scale would be no criterion of relative merit; and yet we find at least one able writer so enamored by the British upper and middle class that he manages on eugenic grounds to find reasons for the main-

<hr />

[3] For a vigorous arraignment of British imperialism of the year 1903 see: *Democracy and Reaction,* chapter 2.

tenance of class distinctions."[4] Of the qualities that bring economic success in modern society some are good and some bad. The general structure of social organization and control will determine which type of qualities are allowed to attain success and recognition. Our descendants may regard great financiers of today much as we regard the robber barons of old.

Some of the political eugenists go very far in condemning social reform as overturning the laws of natural selection and the survival of the fit. That social progress is the antithesis of natural selection is a central point in the Hobhouse social theory. His position is set forth in detail in the chapter dealing with pre-human adaptation in the evolutionary process. To the specific contention that the race is doomed unless we immediately alter our institutions to encourage the propagation of the fit and to prevent the propagation of the unfit, he replies that the race is at present on the up grade. Moreover, he maintains that in England the fall in the death rate, the rise of real wages, and the decline of pauperism,—all make doubtful such a contention.

Hobhouse makes two suggestions for a rational eugenic program. Biological emphasis being placed upon the great significance of mutations, a rational eugenic program should go about establishing an environment in which socially useful mutations would have every chance to develop. Again, it may turn out that mental and moral differences are due to differences in proportion. "It is quite possible then that two strains, each sound in itself, should when united produce a bad result, and it may turn out that the true problem of eugenics is not of selective breeding but of selective mating."[5]

[4] *Social Evolution and Political Theory,* p. 47.
[5] *Ibid.,* pp. 69-70.

It is clear that Hobhouse expects progress to come through social rather than racial changes; he views with unqualified disapproval the contentions of extreme eugenists (who in America would be represented by men like Mr. Wiggam) ; finally, he has certain hopes of a mild eugenic program, if it is applied with great caution.

Rights and *duties* are natural corollaries of moral freedom which makes purposive conduct possible. Wherever one browses in the writings of Hobhouse he will not long pursue his reading before encountering the ever recurring theme of "purpose" in the direction of world affairs. His philosophic discussion of free-will and moral responsibility is detailed and closely reasoned. It will not be gone over; it is enough to recall that freedom and responsibility are fundamental to his social theory and that the freedom of the individual is basic to all other freedom.

Much confusion arises regarding freedom and this Hobhouse tries to clear up. It has been suggested that every man should have full liberty provided he does not interfere with the same liberty of another man. Yet if A is a pugilist and B an ordinary man there is no justice in such a proposition; whatever happens to liberty, acknowledged rights of the individual must be preserved. Where two wills clash the choice between them should rest on the best judgment of the community as to which makes the larger contribution to the common welfare. Wherever there is a conflict some liberty must be restricted, though a certain amount of liberty is essential to character. In our society today, imperfect and badly formed as it is, the ability to tolerate differences is the basis of the highest harmony. And even if finality in the theory of life were possible men would need to accept it through freedom rather than coercion. In proportion as an individual varies from type he has the chance of contributing something to the common good.   Coercion pauperizes reason in forcing it to surrender its work to absolute force.

One of the difficult problems in connection with individual freedom is that of free contract. The stronger party to a bargain may impose disastrous terms upon the weaker, hence the modern state has intervened to prevent such injustice. To speak of such state-action as a curtailment of liberty is a mere abstraction; there are other rights of the individual not less important than the right of free contract. Again freedom of contract is too briefly defined as mere absence of control. "For by Liberty . . . we mean the open field for mind and character, and the rights that we maintain and the restrictions that we impose should so far as compatible with other conditions of social organization be conceived in the interest of such development."[6]

What shall we say, asks Hobhouse, when *law* and *conscience* come into conflict, as with the conscientious objector in war times? If we may assume a situation in which the community honestly believes that the service of every individual is necessary, then it is justified in coercing the individual. It has no right, however, to treat him as a common criminal, but rather, as a martyr. There are religious bodies not believing in the reality of disease and such groups might spread infection. That the state in coercing them is acting for the will of the community is of course a large assumption. In modern times the state's activities have tended toward a better protection of personal rights, as in the economic sphere, and the organization of public resources for common enterprises like education and unemployment insurance. This does not involve a loss of liberty nor a mulcting of one class to benefit another, as in making

[6] *Elements of Social Justice,* p. 85.

the rich pay for the education of the poor, but is an appropriation for common use of wealth arising out of common effort. It is one aspect of liberty that the immature should receive proper training,—the child has a right to the education that may bring its mind to maturity. While force is necessary in society as now constituted, the whole effort of social planning should be pointed toward replacing force by a fundamental harmony resting on right and reason. One of the surest ways of securing this is by keeping wide open the channels of criticism.

The precept "all men are by nature equal" may be interpreted in two ways; either that nature endows with equal innate capacity all individuals, which is untrue, or that all have equal rights, and this merits examination. Every being that can feel has rights in the sense that he is entitled to consideration. Where special obligations arise the principle of equality insists that it shall apply equally to all falling under the special obligations. Equality from the stand point of differences is an adjustment in which these differences are made a basis of varying treatment.

Schematically Hobhouse has set down his views as follows:

"1. By equality is meant equality of proportion between claims and satisfaction.

"2. Claims are based either on need or desert. On the one view equal needs, on the other equal desert requires equal satisfaction.

"3. Desert may be measured by effort or attainment. These principles are of general application. But further, men are born or enter into special relations to particular people. In regard to these equality means:

"4. (a) Equal reciprocal obligation on all parties to the relation of equal cogency.

(b) Equal opportunity to all to enter into such special relations as are constituted by human choice."[7]

Certain kinds of equality are maintained by law and others at present are thwarted by it. Now a law is a universal rule impartially applied to all who fall under it and in most modern states rules are framed treating certain fundamental rights and duties applying to all human beings. The impartiality of the law may be criticised on ethical grounds in that the individual cases falling under one classification vary enormously. Members of the community, simply as members, have basically equal claims on the common good; the differences in what any individual receives must be based on differences required by the common good. *Needs* vary in two ways: in *quantity,* as to satisfy hunger one man requires more than another; in *urgency,*—a minimum of food and clothing being more necessary than an added quantity. The law of diminishing returns applies here rigorously. "Differences arise in a system in which all have a part, and a claim to equal consideration, from the necessities of the system itself."[8] Distributive justice is defined; there must always be an equal satisfaction of equal needs, subject always to an adequate maintenance of useful functions.

Some writers hold that the development of a few to a high point is far more important than a slight development for the great mass. Hobhouse naturally maintains that this errs in taking development in the abstract rather than development in harmony as a measure of value. Yet there is something cringing in human nature that accounts for its fascination by a figure like Napoleon. The community has paid a heavy price for the contribution that superior classes have

[7] *Ibid.,* p. 113.
[8] *Ibid.,* p. 124.

made to the work of civilization if such superiority has rested upon subordination of less capable groups. For "the rational good is one in which all persons share in proportion to the capacity of their social personality. This is the fundamental principle of proportionate equality in the Common Good, the governing conception of social justice."[9] Further, along the same line, it is objected that the material conditions for a good life are not available for all and if this is true would it not be better for the *good life* to be attained by some, though impossible for all. The war and the blockade brought the nations of Europe to face this question.

From this situation certain principles of action emerged. First, if it were a question of insufficiency, all must go short except that soldiers be well fed. When faced with the necessity of preserving the common life, every community turned to equality, due allowance being made always for maintaining necessary common functions. Second, when actual starvation was faced children and the aged and infirm were cared for as being the more necessitous and dependent, and the hope of the community. Third, if the point is reached where either some must die or all must die (as on a torpedoed ship) equality fails simply because it is no longer physically possible. Two riders to the doctrine of equality must be added: first, evil is lessened and good enhanced by sharing; second, where necessities are short, superfluities must vanish. There is vast difference in degree between the simpler comforts and the more elaborate luxuries; "The workman's pipe is worth more to him than the collection of rare gems to the millionaire. It is easily deduced that, except, perhaps, in an enormously rich society, the social value of material wealth tends to increase as the distribution becomes more

---

[9] *Ibid.*, p. 133.

equable."[10] To apply such a system of equality in the world as it is leads immediately to a consideration of individual rewards and punishments.

The very kernel of the problem of justice consists in finding individual merit and giving it its due. Yet how are we to compare the deserts of the honest and industrious but incompetent man with those of the efficient man? There are two extreme positions here, we are assured, and both are equally false. According to one a man is the sole bearer of the consequences of his acts, but this is an impossible individualism. According to the other, virtue and vice each bring their own sufficient consequences, and this implies an impossible socialism.

Regarding differences in reward it is clear that these must be at bottom sufficient to repay the individual for losses of energy involved in carrying out the required function. As to punishment it is sometimes held that the evil ought to fall as far as possible upon the offender; this view conceives of wrongdoing as spiritual or magical in character. The offender may of his own good will allow the wrath of the gods to fall upon his own head and thus redeem himself and save society. Rationally, we cannot wish evil as such to the offender. Society must protect itself and this may involve threats and prison sentences. The reaction of society to the criminal is justified only as a means to its own safety and must have the good of the criminal in view so far as the conditions to this safety allows. To inflict punishment for the good of the offender is an inversion of the true order of motives. The good of the offender would palliate or modify the shape and form of the evil inflicted for the good of society; thinking of the welfare of the criminal should modify the evil inflicted for the good of society. For one thing, if there existed

[10] *Ibid.,* pp. 136-137.

a more equable system of making payment for services rendered to society there would be fewer criminals to punish.

One is inclined to say that the simple rule of justice as applied to exchange is that values given and taken should be equal. Yet this requires careful examination. Both buyer and seller should benefit by the transaction, not one at the expense of the other. Of course a transaction in modern society is not an isolated exchange; it is a link in the chain of production and distribution of wealth. It must be judged as it effects the whole process. Social intelligence should be turned to meeting the needs of all members of the community in relation to the urgency of the needs. Always with the proviso that necessary economic functions are maintained. Moreover, neither functionless wealth nor the opportunity of earning income by socially injurious or useless work should be tolerated; wealth should be acquired only by social service. Further, the smallest compensation society should allow to its least skilled necessary worker should be sufficient to maintain him in a condition of full civic efficiency. Though at present the least skilled do not earn the minimum, in a competitive system earnings depend not on power to work but power of getting paid for it. In our capitalistic society the poorer a man is the smaller his chances of escaping from poverty.

However, this brings us to a serious question. What proportion of workers would be excluded from employment in a given industry if their remuneration, on the basis of actual social earnings, was required to come up to the established minimum? Whenever wages are increased there is always the threat of excluding a certain percentage of workers. Experience shows the number actually excluded to be small. The reason? Any increase in wages up to the minimum brings a sharp rise in the workers' efficiency. Again, the notion of a civic minimum is often questioned. For, it is held, if everyone is entitled to the minimum, even the criminal, is it not mockery to tell the unskilled worker that he is earning what he would receive in any case? The answer is, a man's earnings are his own for free disposal; what the criminal or defective receives is for a specific purpose and the community exercises full control. Increases above the minimum are required for every additional unit of effort whether due to the arduousness of the work or the increased application of the worker.

If the civic minimum is to be applied, it is indicated, many things must be analyzed. In deciding vital costs the total situation must be considered. Due allowance must be made for the cost of training. When we face a comparison of degrees of skill there is real difficulty. In any existing economic system reward is most uneven and the best social work is usually unpaid. The tale of the starving genius of art is too familiar to need retelling. One theory suggests that the producer is entitled to the whole value of his product. This, however, is an imperfect analysis of a social system where the exact value of any labor is almost impossible to determine. Again, it is argued that a person should do his full duty by society because it is his duty. Yet, taking human nature as it evidently is, some measure of recognition and payment on the basis of accomplishment rather than effort does promote achievement. To the question whether such differentiation is just it is replied that society owes to a man not only opportunity to useful service but also opportunity to shape his life in his own way. In this he may enrich himself by his own efforts if society is also enriched.

It is easy to set the common good over against the individual good in sharp antithesis, but such a division is generally unreal. If the individual is made to give up his additional wealth, oftentimes it goes to a rather stupid and commonplace government; one that may use it in building up a great war machine. Some individuals would put it to more intelligent use, as in experiments with new ideas.

If remuneration is to be related to *value,* how is *value* in the last analysis to be decided? In several ways. Where we are concerned with different amounts of the same good remuneration is simply on the piece work basis, provided no one is pushed below the civic minimum. Between different kinds of work we must turn to the law of demand and supply as touching available ability. If we ask what is really high grade ability, the answer is that it has high value in use and that it is difficult to obtain. Of course demand and supply are not ethical principles but they are operative facts. That is to say, given payment by value of output, demand and supply measure the varying values of commodities of different qualities. A dentist's income would be determined by the skill of his work and the number of other dentists in his community. The maximum allowable remuneration for services can be determined by experience of the amount of wealth which it is desirable for the community to allow any individual to hold. Under the conditions indicated a system of free exchange is desirable.

Once private exchange and private property are conceded by Hobhouse other nettlesome problems clamor for handling. How far shall the individual be allowed to "do as he will with his own"? What of the oppressive power that often comes to the individual through the mere fact of ownership?

All property is limited by the universal rights of other people. Social control must enforce this; property is a form of regulated control. The antithesis of property is not socialistic ownership but anarchistic communism. For what is not property may be used or misused by anyone. Common use and enjoyment are possible only where misuse cannot take place or where it can easily be checked. Being a form of control, property carries a certain liberty and a certain responsibility. The responsibility is involved in self-dependence. Individuals and corporate bodies that must direct their own affairs require some property. Yet this should not go so far as to give such power over other persons as falls to the owner of an intervening strip of land desired by the community for a roadway or other improvement.

If wealth is unevenly distributed it gives its possessor, as an employer, undue advantage in making a contract with a worker. Hence in modern industry there is great unfreedom in the dependence of the worker on the owner of the means of production—the tools with which he must make a living. Of course society may, in attempting to reach economic freedom, set up the peasant proprietor and the one-man business. But in a highly industrialized society these have a diminishing place. The alternative is to establish wealth as a social function absolutely dependent on social control. For property, as economic power, must in the last resort rest in the self governing community. The individual cannot be allowed limitless *power* but he may be given much of the *freedom* that goes with property.

Economic power leads to liberty if the individual, on the basis of his capacity, can have a voice in the collective decisions affecting the total social structure of which he is a part. The industrial government must assure every individual capable of working a right to work, to obtain advancement by merit, and to enjoy one of the rewards of service which is personal property. Also, the worker must be able to provide against sickness, old age, accident, unemployment, and all those things that drag many down into pauperism. Hobhouse thus endorses a very wide application of social insurance to be financed by the community. All of which means that the amount of wealth owned outright by the community, to carry through its social insurance, will be greatly increased.

The community, it is pointed out, may claim ownership of wealth on two grounds. In the first place, the community performs certain functions which require due return. There is the organization to bring about security, including that of property itself. The state organization is used to increase the value of property by measures for social progress, and these may return nothing to the state directly,—as the installation of a drainage system. The individual is often enriched by social efforts to which he contributes nothing, and most individual production is in large part social production. Now if the social factor of wealth does not get its proportionate return, mal-adjustment results. As the industry of a town expands, rents are forced up, and the "ground landlord" skims off all the cream of values which is a result of complex congeries of social factors. If these same values came back to the town the increased population would pay its way. There would be available resources for building, for beautifying the town and for carrying through countless civic projects. English towns have been starved of their natural revenues and are ugly, crowded, and mean. Yet not alone for performing services may the community claim a right to property.

In the second place, the community may rightly claim all property not directly belonging either to individuals or to social organizations. Natural resources would normally fall in this group. There must be some reason for giving the individual ownership of any property, since it gives rights to one individual as against another. With Hobhouse the only claims recognized here are a clear need or a function performed. Neither of these holds true of private property in natural resources or, generally speaking, of inherited property.

Functionless wealth, in contrast with wealth that serves the community, grows easily where the individual may inherit a fortune or own a coal mine. Many arguments have been advanced to support both the ownership of natural resources and the passing on of fortunes from father to son. Most popular perhaps is the contention that economic functions are better fulfilled by private individuals than by public ownership. If this is true it is because of default by the community; and it is contended that it has not been established as true. Inheritance and bequest have a function so long as the community does not provide thoroughly for the young and helpless. Inheritance has also been defended as a stimulus to production and accumulation. Defenders of the capitalist system point out that the bulk of yearly savings comes from the large surplus incomes of rich individuals and it is assumed that savings would cease if there were not these large fortunes. This takes it for granted that the community lacks the sense and means to save. Yet on the basis of sound economy a more wasteful method of securing accumulation could hardly be devised than the one now used.

There is however a more human argument for inheritance and it cannot be ignored. "Parents cannot brook the thought that any child may for want of effort on their part be forced to live on a standard to which it has not been brought up."[11] A valuable human impulse is thwarted if due provision cannot be made for children. The main duty is education, for which due provisions should certainly be made by the community.

[11] *Ibid.*, p. 193.

Yet many problems arise, such as the cruelty of cutting off a parent from providing very careful treatment for a delicate child. Parents know the needs of children in a way that a public system cannot. However, the fact remains that for children to live on inheritance is to use functionless wealth.

In this dilemma Hobhouse makes an amazing suggestion. It is that if a parent wishes to provide for his child he be allowed to do so by gifts during his life rather than by bequest. This is defended on the ground that parental feeling, and desire to found a family are two distinct things and the later would be thwarted if inheritances were abolished. Why Hobhouse believes people of means would not quickly and effectively adjust to the new situation is not indicated. The skill of many in dodging present inheritance taxes is to the point. However, his position could be made tenable in modified form by the added provision that no parent could transfer to his child property in excess of a specified amount. Law might further provide that property not so transferred should revert to the community at death, with the exception of personal objects such as furniture and books. From the standpoint of tax gathering, this seems workable.

In a thoroughgoing discussion of weath, we are told, a fundamental distinction must be drawn between social and unsocial elements in wealth. In pure economics the question as to whether production is social or unsocial is of minor interest, but it is a fundamental question in the ethics of property and industry. An unsanitary house is a source of wealth to the owner but is socially a liability. The social value of many other items in a nation's production would vary with the amount consumed. With alcohol there would be vast differences of opinion as to how much consumption is desirable. All would agree, however, that the maximum point of production and consumption is handsomely passed in England. In the ideal statistics of social welfare here imagined all production that passed this hypothetical point would figure as a minus quantity, because, ethically speaking, production and distribution of wealth are conditioned by the function of wealth as a basis of social life. Actual production and distribution may be guided so that all wealth is social wealth.

Wealth, then, may be social or unsocial, and, furthermore, there are social and unsocial methods of acquiring wealth. It is possible for a clever bartering individual to add to his own riches without making an addition to the wealth of society. The buying and selling of stocks, the broker maintains, may be regarded as a payment for the regulation of industry. With equal justice it may be viewed, according to Hobhouse, as a tax upon society because of its poor organization. Here it seems that society might reduce the profit through aiding the better organization of industry, and through taxation increase the degree of foresight required to make the business of financial middleman profitable. Again, through exchange the advantage goes to the stronger purchaser. The qualities of the bargainer are antisocial and the results accruing to the individual are in reality a tax on others. Except as it is dependent on differences of organizing ability the possession of differential advantages in production may have an unsocial effect. "We arrive at the conclusion that profit on price, except so far as it results from socially serviceable qualities such as able organization, is wealth to the individual which makes no net addition to the wealth of the whole community."[12]

Profit-taking is ethical if it is given as payment for social service. This is true provided the community has

[12] *Ibid.*, p. 200.

brought about fair treatment of employees and the elimination of antisocial methods of gain and provided the community allows no profits on inherited capital. Of course, if private enterprise is eliminated and prices are fixed the community may take over the entire surplus and private enterprise must prove itself so far superior to such a system that it overcomes this differential return to the community.

Whatever the system of collecting the surplus, its utilization presents many problems. Raising the civic minimum of the worker through providing gratuitously and universally certain necessary elements of the minimum has much to recommend it. The cost of producing any given commodity varies enormously from place to place. It is rational to make up a portion of the wage out of the social surplus accumulated by the community. Certain needs such as education and sanitation should never be stinted and they will not be if the community adequately provides them for all. Yet the question remains: is private profit as such ethical?

Against production by private profit there are two main ethical arguments. It is held in the first place that the "reward of management" is irregular and unequal. To this Hobhouse replies that to balance the risk of enterprise there is joy of ownership; that there is a type of individual who prefers risk and adventure, and, finally, that such a type under proper safeguards has social value. In the second place it is held that the profit motive is a low motive. The reply is, that though social service is a higher motive, it does not appeal to all men; that with a chance for profit man takes the risk of failure. Moreover, even though profit is a poor motive, it is a valuable economic check. In private enterprise the books *must* balance but this is not true in community enterprises. In some forms of production there is no great superiority of one method over the other; whether public or private production is used the individual case must be examined to determine.

To replace private management certain methods are often suggested. First, we may have management by state or municipality. On the whole, Hobhouse maintains, this has been a success and might be extended to such things as the production of milk, coal, bread, and similiar commodities in general demand. State management of transportation has not been highly successful, due in part to the routine traditions of the civil service. Here also there is the difficulty of securing popular control of a national bureaucracy which may easily become the master of the people. However it is not an impossible situation and just as we have secured an honest civil service it might be possible to secure an enterprising and popularly controlled one.

In the second place society might replace private management by industrial self-government through coöperative guilds. Under such a scheme each industry would be organized on a world-wide basis and would determine the policies of that particular industry. A congress of guilds would determine the relations between the guilds, and a special body representing the consumers would be present. This for Hobhouse would be a tempered form of monopoly, with vast power in the hands of the guilds,—particularly in such key industries as coal mining and railway work. Unless some method of preventing this undue concentration of power can be devised the general scheme is regarded as undesirable.

In the third place we might have industrial organization by the consumer and the consumer's coöperatives. This has had remarkable success within limits but is could not solve the general industrial problem. It is at the opposite pole from guild socialism in that it does nothing for the producer as such. It began in the retail trade and has *worked back;* in other fields of industry it has made no sensible mark.

Failing these methods there are various suggestions to modify private enterprise even though it be not replaced. There is the possibility of dealing with the coal mines, for example, as set forth in the Sankey report. This is a promising lead, Hobhouse holds, and is worth going over. A body is set up representing producers and consumers; among the producers there are two sections, workers and managers; among the consumers, representatives of householders and industrial consumers. While there might seem to be a deadlock between the two divisions there is actually a three-fold division,—consumers, management, and technical staff. Whether such a scheme be tried or some other, there are certain basic principles of industry not to be forgotten.

A sharp line is to be drawn between the *managerial function* of directing industry, and the *labor conditions* under which the worker lives. Labor conditions, the management must accept. These are to be determined judicially by representatives of the community with a jury or impartial element to decide controversial points. This in general is the Trade Board method. The government in Great Britain has tried on occasion to act both as executive and judge, functions not compatible. One problem of great complexity is to give the worker the fixity of tenure to which he is entitled along with the mobility required in a world of ever shifting industry. Yet underlying all other problems in modern society is one great question: how can an effective democracy be developed? Industrial readjustments are but small phases of the general social process, and how such process is to be made democratic is an unsolved riddle.

Normally the life of mankind is in a sense democratic, even in a slave system. The ultimate root of the democratic principle is recognition that if one is to be free all must be free. Yet freedom is relative, and a man's freedom is always conditioned by the equal claims of others. Politically, every man's will must be taken into account. This is the unsolved problem of political democracy. Mere voting is of little effect for the voter cannot be consulted about everything. Practically he can only function in certain critical decisions. The difficulty of democracy is then not so much a bad or a selfish will but to get any will at all that is coherent.

Some place great store by majority rule but there is much of chance in determining who gets the majority. Some of the defects of majority rule as it ordinarily functions today might be removed by proportional representation; in any event majority rule must be exercised with caution. It may be tolerated in a homogeneous population, but where race, religion, color, or nationality divide the population it is intolerable. To tell a small close-knit minority that it must submit in any event because the majority rules against it is not democracy but oligarchy. One might add that in America the majority ordinarily tells its racial minority "if you don't like American institutions as they are you can go back where you came from," which by no stretch of the imagination could be called democracy as here considered.

Democracy implies besides liberty and equality a synthetic principle, the community. That is, all differences within the body are minor compared to the more comprehensive agreement; they are family differences. With proper safe-guards two entirely different communities may form a state but not through simple majority rule. Whether any uniting of diverse nationali-

ties into a state will be successful depends partly upon
the scrupulous honesty with which the terms of agreement are kept. The union of England with Scotland,
and of England with Ireland is illuminating. On this
matter Mr. Hobhouse feels strongly. "Put more bru-
tally, the Anglo-Scottish Union was based on a compact (commercial union) which was kept. The British-
Irish Union was based on a compact (Catholic Eman-
cipation) which for twenty-eight years was broken."[13]

Where a nationality inhabits a distinct territory internal autonomy should be the rule. Sense of community
should also cause a common feeling to prevail when
some section of it is subjected to peculiar suffering.
During the World War the stoicism with which men
and women comfortably situated in England bore up
against the hardships of trench warfare was a feature
of the national character which brough about daily
self-congratulation. "When in October 1918 it became
a question whether we should relieve the actual suf-
ferers—our own sons and brothers—or enjoy a spec-
tacular victory, there was no doubt as to the preference
of popular emotion. It was all for more vicarious
heroism."[14] True sense of community had here failed.

The real community sense is confused by theories
of the state now obsolete. If we postulate a certain
sense of community but with it a certain feeling of dis-
community, then we come to the theory of the sovereign
state. In its extreme form this leads to the God-State of
Hegel. The Idealists of the Hegelian school look about
for a superpersonal entity in society in which the individual may find most complete self-realization, and this
entity is found in the state. Only by merging himself
in the state, it is held, does the individual realize his
greatest possibilities. The chief duty therefore of every

[13] *Ibid.*, p. 227.
[14] *Ibid.*, p. 228.

individual is complete acquiescence in the will of the State. The State on the other hand has no obligations to the world outside. It is judged only by the process of world history. To all of which Hobhouse replies that the state is only one of the social institutions to which man owes loyalty. The family, art, science, and ingrained notions of right and wrong, to mention only a few, often set up loyalties cutting across and making quite impossible the unquestioning loyalty to the state desired by the idealist.

The idealist philosophy, in the opinion of Hobhouse, does not strive to realize the ideal but rather to idealize the real. Thus for the idealist any attempt to establish a rational order in society would be a mere "fantasy of the subjective reason," since the state as it exists is far better than any which could be worked out by rational thought. We are then to accept the world as it is and try to appreciate it. To which Hobhouse replies that only the social satirist could treat this foolish idea adequately.[15]

The same idealist philosophy is evidenced in milder form in the theory of sovereignty. According to the current popular notion, after the vote has been taken the rights of the minority cease. There *must* be action; the majority rules. Historically this theory goes back to authoritarian conceptions of kingship. In democracy

[15] For a statement of the Hegelian theory of the state together with a vigorous arraignment of it see Hobhouse's *The Metaphysical Theory of the State, a Criticism,* 1918.   This little volume of lectures was written during war time and is not entirely free from the violent emotions of that period.   Both here and in his other writings of the period he indicates that Germany took her first fatal step toward militarism when the Hegelian notions of the state began to find credence.   Once they were accepted, logical development led to a militant Germany demanding her place in the sun.   Here we see Hobhouse the philosopher turning to philosophy for an explanation of historic events.   This is not a unique thing in his writings but might rather be spoken of as typical.

government becomes the servant and the people the master, but essentially the same ancient king-and-people relation holds for the minority. This doctrine of absolutism was combated by the constitutionalists from Paine to Mill. Mill contended that the individual only gave up to the state such things as were necessary for collective organization. There were many rights the state could not invade; "A man's house is his castle," etc.

The concept of absolute sovereignty in the state will not stand under analysis. In the democratic community there is no assignable person or group exercising absolute power; the people act through some organ and there is none which entirely prescribes its will. The notion of the sovereign state indicates the final authority of a politically organized community with independence from others. This puts loyalty to state outside the moral law and patriotism above humanity. This, together with fear of war and necessity of armament, has tended to make the modern state a great hate-organization.[16] Ethically, there is only one ultimate community, the human race. Though it has not found organized expression, it is an obligation of statesmanship to bring it about. Meanwhile the world fellow-feeling has been represented imperfectly by various organized bodies, as of states, churches, and scientific associations. These foreshadow the world community.

To bring about rational world adjustments a world organization is needed. One possibility is to establish a functional society, as previously mentioned. The different duties to be performed, such as coal mining, would be organized on a world basis. There would then be a world congress of guilds to regulate the necessary work of society. It has been argued in support of

[16] *Elements of Social Justice*, p. 240.

this that the coal miners in different portions of the world could intelligently coöperate on problems relating to their own work while they might be wholly ignorant regarding some problem of educational procedure. This concept of social organization is still in the plastic stage. It is mainly criticised on the ground that those performing a function are likely to forget the real purpose of that function. The direction of education should not be left entirely to teachers. Hobhouse suggests: "It is probably necessary to the effective union of humanity, since we cannot overcome division, that it should be divided on different principles at the same time, so that men who are opposed in one relation find themselves coöperating in another."[17]

If functional government were secured on the right basis, Hobhouse maintains, there would be with each function certain things that appeal strongly to those performing it. This would bring about a better public spirit than the confused appeals of politics today. In any event an organ of justice would be required and other adequate means of coördinating the various functions. Any world league established should include international functions as well as states.

The world organization visualized by Hobhouse is vastly different from the present League of Nations. He states: "However, . . . if democracy is to succeed—or for that matter if civilization is to survive—the present aborted embryo called the League of Nations must develop in the direction of an international Federation."[18] The World league must limit state sovereignty and decide interstate questions, limit armaments, guarantee free commercial intercourse, assure elementary rights of the individual and act as a court between any state and recalcitrant nationalties in

[17] *Ibid.*, p. 239.
[18] *Ibid.*, p. 240.

its boundaries. With these limitations the state may continue the regulation of organizations performing the principal functions of self government. The state will determine the established relations between industries in any given territory whether or not it ever organized the mass of industry as contemplated in the functional view of society. Such state regulation of industry would be subject, of course, to the general conditions established by the League of Nations.

Looking back over the actual proposals of Hobhouse for dealing with present world problems it becomes increasingly clear that he belongs with the "Left Wing" of the British Liberal Party. He has left behind his earlier socialism which led him as a college boy to throw himself into the effort to organize the agricultural workers about Oxford. Yet he has not left it far behind, and one suspects that his real distaste for political socialism grows out of his natural feeling toward such phrases as "the dictatorship of the proletariat" and "class solidarity," and toward the frequent use of the word Revolution. The freedom of thought of Liberalism is more congenial than doctrinaire Socialism. Socialism as ordinarily understood includes much of dogma unnecessary to it theoretically,—as also the strong class hatred often found with it,—and not a part of its broad theory of collective control. These things hardly make good bed-fellows with the idea of an evolving rational harmony; a harmony toward which we inevitably move but that may be speeded up through intelligent effort.

Man's best collective effort, Hobhouse points out, should be directed toward eliminating maladjustments in the world today. Imperialism should be recognized as the naked taking of what is wanted by fair means or foul and is to be thoroughly condemned because it inevitably brings a violation of the rights of nationality. Of course *rights* are generally relative to the whole situation in which they are claimed to exist; and the claim to nationality in one group may not be allowed to destroy the vital rights of another group. A similar situation holds for the rights of the individual within the community, though equality can only be approximated in a world of human beings. The development of one class at the expense of another, however, is never justified. Vast wealth for the few and poverty for the many is consequently unthinkable in the truly ethical social order. Wealth concentration may be largely checked through eliminating functionless wealth; stopping inheritance, and checking profit from socially useless work. Yet the wealth acquired by the individual even under these circumstances cannot be regarded as his own exclusive property but must be severely regulated by the community in the interest of all. The *power* growing naturally out of property should rest entirely in the community, but the *freedom* it brings belongs to the individual. Whether property used in the industrial organization can be directed most intelligently by the individual or the community depends upon a variety of factors, but provision of the common necessities like bread and milk might well be in the hands of the community. The type of political organization best adapted to carrying through these functions is not the sovereign state, with its ideas of absolutism, but a political grouping that is one unit in a world state. A functional organization of the world community is one possibility of the future that holds out promise.

In this brief chapter a wide range of material has been brought under review and the Hobhousian concepts in many fields of thought narrated. From individual rights and personal ethics to international relations and the possible future world community is a long journey. Truly sociology when handled by a master is synthetic! We have dealt particularly with basic concepts of political science, economics, ethics and psychology. To attempt detailed criticism of such a vast array of ideas will not be here attempted. Certain incidental criticisms have found their way into the text and some of the concepts treated in other chapters were there examined in detail. However, it may clarify the Hobhouse concepts if they are brought into relation with certain other concepts.

In political science his ideas of sovereignty have much in common with Laski and are sharply opposed to the views of the traditional political scientist. In practical politics he might theoretically be classified as Left-Wing Liberal, or a follower of the moderates of the British Labour Party, as you choose. In Economics many of his views agree closely with those of J. A. Hobson. In ethics he is entirely himself. He writes against the background of his early religious training and his rational philosophy. Where similar topics are touched in social ethics, he sometimes parallels John Dewey, sometimes disagrees. In psychology Hobhouse is a cautious introspectionist. As to individual motivation it is difficult to judge how much reliance he places upon the psychoanalytic approach. He mentions somewhere the genuine contributions recently made to morbid psychology but it is in connection with a warning against fads in science.

These suggestions, however, are simply "guides" for the blind; they are not intended as classificatory categories. The writings of Hobhouse, as of most great thinkers, cannot be fitted into neatly labeled pigeonholes.

VI. SOCIOLOGY AS A SCIENCE

During the last half century the treatment of social problems by serious scholars has enormously increased. The natural result has been the development of various techniques for handling different aspects of these problems. The consequence of the revolt against earlier brilliant but untenable generalizations growing out of the philosophy of history has been a constantly narrowing specialization. Certain problems are primarily political, others economic, others biological, and others historical. Psychological theory underlies all of them. Any main heading yields an endless number of subdivisions; specialties legitimately arise. In such a situation does not the position of the sociologist become increasing untenable? How can one be concerned with the entire social process in a scientific way when someone else's specialization is covering every particular aspect of the broad field? The answer of Hobhouse to these questions is interesting.

Psychologically considered Hobhouse thinks of sociology as a product of the interaction of minds. "Essentially the subject-matter of sociology is the interaction of individual minds."[1] For Hobhouse, sociological method must be a synthesis of philosophical and scientific method. This has been referred to previously and has become increasingly clear as we have run over the main points of his social theory. Now while the sociologist must inevitably give certain hostages to philosophy whenever he suggests any improvement in society, it seems clear that the more rigidly these philosophical assumptions can be limited the more sub-

[1] *Social Development,* p. 11.

stantial the foundation of social theory will be. Consequently in the present volume the philosophical positions of Hobhouse are not treated in detail. In his discussion of the place of the sociologist his predilection for philosophy is again made evident.

Considerable attention is devoted to the apparent conflict between free will in the individual and a science of society. How can the *units* of a group in a measure be free to choose one course rather than another and the course of the group's evolution in any sense be predictable? One solution of this problem is suggested as lying in the law of probability. If a large number of individuals are entirely free to choose between A and B, then, unless other factors than those of their freedom enter into consideration, about half will choose A and the other half B. Consequently on the assumption of free will we may expect any general drift or tendency to be due not to the individual's freedom but to other factors. It is the business of the sociologist to discover and evaluate these other factors. It follows then from the standpoint of probability that a law of social causation is likely to be carried through in direct proportion to the number of persons involved. This would follow exactly as would the probability of securing an equal number of 'heads' and 'tails' from the toss of a coin; that is, the probability would be greater for one hundred throws than for fifty.

Yet have we a right to speak of social or economic *laws?* For Hobhouse the answer to this question is, emphatically, yes. When science discovers certain relations that hold uniformly these are called laws. Yet most if not all of these laws indicate that certain consequences follow certain conditions. If any of the conditions fail to be present in a given situation, the law does not hold. When we attempt to apply the law to actual situations in the world, it holds only approximately. The law of gravity cannot be treated by simple formula when we must consider variations in atmospheric pressure. The fact that law is an approximation, however, does not prevent its use in the control of nature. In the same way a social law, like that of demand and supply, can be explained theoretically in relation to the price of any commodity. However, it rests upon certain assumptions, as that the individual will buy his commodity where he can secure it most cheaply and sell his commodity (usually his labor) at the highest price he can secure. Whenever these assumptions fail to hold, the law is not invalidated though it is not in operation. It holds when the conditions hold. Scientific law is not broken, yet expectations in any concrete situation may not be fulfilled. This is due to some condition to the law's operation not being present.

Laws hold in society as they do in medicine. A person's life during the course of a severe illness may depend upon the presence or absence of a noise nearby. No one can predict whether the patient will live or die. This does not mean that medicine has no scientific basis. Again, no one can predict whether an apparently normal individual will die of pneumonia at twenty or live to be an octogenarian. What can be stated with assurance is that if the individual allows his resistance to fall below a certain point and if other conditions are met he will contract pneumonia, the prognosis will be bad, and he will very probably die. It can also be predicted that by complying with certain other conditions the individual enormously increases his probability of living to a ripe old age. Similarly in society the greater social causes hold. "Grant that the Great War would not have broken out if in July, 1914, the minds of half a dozen men had been other than they were— had even temporarily been swayed by other motives. Would this petty alteration have sensibly dissipated the vast cloud of distrust which overshadowed Europe?"[2] Science can discover the broad tendencies of social life and formulate laws concerning them. Every society has its own history yet this does not prevent it conforming to general laws applicable to all societies.

If on the one hand Hobhouse will not allow free will to block the development of social science, on the other hand he denies emphatically that man is simply a reacting mechanism and that social evolution runs along a predetermined course. He states, "the analysis of sociological laws completely dissipates this fatalistic view. It reveals in society no superhuman monster but simply human beings, human minds and bodies, human wills and passion, in interaction with one another and the physical environment. There can be no laws in question but (1) those of the human soul, (2) those of the interactions of human beings one with another, and (3) those of the consequences of such actions."[3]

So far the discussion of sociology as a science or a possible science has been in rather general terms. One naturally inquires what specific methods Hobhouse has used in his own extensive research. Throughout his writing very great attention is concentrated upon the philosophical justification for any positions taken. Social philosophy, which proposes to find a coherent scheme of social betterment, is treated in detail. Primary importance from a scientific point of view is attached to his psychological analysis and research. His views in psychology together with the results of his studies have been set forth elsewhere. In this field he is a follower of MacDougall. His psychological experiments, carried on a quarter of a century ago, could not be accepted as a valid basis for generalizations today. His psychological analysis of group behavior which he

[2] *Social Development,* p. 323.
[3] *Ibid.,* p. 325.

considers of primary importance in sociology is both exhaustive and illuminating. Regarding social origins and social evolution he has done three things: followed out in modified form the comparative method of Westermarck and others; given a statistical study of extensive ethnological material; sketched the lines of social evolution during the historic period from the recognized sources.

The weaknesses of the comparative method in ethnology have been discussed elsewhere as have the shortcomings of his statistical treatment of the same material. The comparative method unless used with caution takes facts out of the setting in which they exist. The statistical treatment of ethnological material finds it difficult to establish a satisfactory unit of measurement; it minimizes the significant factor of diffusion; it tends to overlook various qualifying factors such as differences in the density of population.

If one leaves these studies of ethnological material with a feeling that despite the tremendous work put upon them not a great deal has been accomplished, this is happily not true of the studies in social evolution during the period of recorded history. Unusual ability has been shown in the selection of significant facts and the presentation of a relatively brief but coherent sketch of the main phases of social evolution. Undue attention seems to be given to Greece and Rome in this history of culture but no more than is to be expected from one whose early education was based so largely upon a study of the classics. Nevertheless, the lines of social change stand out vividly, and some workable classification of these many changes is of the greatest importance.

The prime object of sociological inquiry for Hobhouse is a social morphology. "Now a social morphology involves not merely a collection of sociological data, but a systematic arrangement of social types, and by social types we mean examples of all the leading forms of human achievement which result from the interaction of individuals,—types of social institution, forms of government, principles of law, types of the family, and, again, intellectual, moral, and artistic traditions, religions, ethical systems, sciences, arts. We need not merely to collect and enumerate the successive achievements of mankind in these various directions, but to arrange them in some way that will exhibit their affinities and interactions, that will help us to appreciate the lines of social development. We need a classification leading up to a social morphology."[4]

One of the prime objects of such a social morphology will be to indicate lines leading back to the origin of any institution or other social form. Of course the *first* form of human marriage will always remain a matter of pure speculation, yet certain relationships may be established between types of marriage and social or economic institutions which will be of fundamental importance.

The work of Hobhouse has been highly diversified. He has written of the intellectual factor in evolution, of the ethical factor in evolution, of a hundred and one specific social ills and how they might be relieved, of psychological experiments, of statistical experiments, of metaphysics, of logic, of many other matters. We venture to predict that his most substantial work lies in social ethics and that for this work he will be longest remembered.

[4] *Social Evolution and Political Theory,* p. 118.

VII. CONCLUSION

The thinking of Hobhouse has had a natural line of growth. The industrious boy who worked diligently upon Latin and Greek passed by easy transitions to philosophy, and the ultimate and the absolute has been important to him since college days. Yet young Hobhouse did not propose to join the philosophers of the ivory tower whose perch was so manifestly insecure. That harmony of the universe which he so much enjoyed, in contemplative mood, evidently required as a preliminary to its complete fulfillment certain readjustments in the workaday world. To those readjustments, or "social reform," he turned naturally. His early efforts in that field disappointed him and threw him back upon his philosophic approach. He decided upon the formulation of a complete code of social ethics and in carrying through that task made a fundamental contribution to social theory. At every point he has buttressed his theoretical code, both by closely reasoned metaphysical discussions—touched lightly in this volume—and by an analysis of practical cases affected by it. As a basis for this code of social ethics he carried through a detailed study of development—mental, societal, and ethical. In the foregoing pages the main outlines of the Hobhousian scheme of thought have been traced, together with certain criticisms. For purposes of clarity the principal points of the outline are repeated here as well as the main aspects of the critical examination of the Hobhousian position. It is hardly necessary to state that there is no pretence to a thorough-going treatment within the restriction of the remaining pages of this chapter.

The first volume from the pen of Hobhouse to attrace wide attention was his *Mind in Evolution*. In the first portion of this book he traces the course of prehuman adaptation in the evolutionary process in so far as *mind* is a factor. Now mind is conceived as the most important factor in the changing and evolving life upon the earth, and long before the level of man is reached it overshadows completely the other factors leading to advance, in the view of Hobhouse. In man the differences between mind and mechanism are so numerous and fundamental as to render the mechanistic interpretation of human conduct entirely untenable. Broadly speaking, man is a free agent using his abilities to size up situations and go about using means toward desired ends that have a high chance of success. To be sure, much of human conduct is mechanically determined, being entirely dependent upon heredity, but in certain critical situations man deliberately chooses his line of conduct. Moreover, a study of behavior in lower organisms indicates clearly that the nearer they approach the level of *homo sapiens* the more evidence they give of such self-determined conduct.

In the lowest organisms we find adjustment to environment brought about through tropism or similar mechanical response. With the beginnings of a true nervous system, organisms come to respond through reflex and instinct. When faced with a situation of food getting or avoidance of danger, the animal does what its ancestors have done for countless generations. Sometimes this response is fatally wrong; the species only manages to maintain itself by breeding an enormous number of young, most of whom perish before reaching maturity. This waste of life can only be avoided when the organism is possessed of a variety of responses any one of which it can call into play as circumstances require. Such a state of things comes about gradually. Elements of it are to be observed before we reach the instinctive response. And as to instinct (here Hobhouse is a bit mystical and metaphysical) the organism possessing nothing higher will sometimes show great ability in solving a strange problem and sometimes very little. However, the hen's maternal instinct gives consistency to her endeavors to care for her brood. It is something which lies at the base of her personality, as it were, and is a foundation for all her activity.

Hobhouse has been much interested in determining the upper levels of intelligence for all animals below man. He carried through detailed, and what must have been time-consuming, experiments, cleverly devised to determine how much of practical judgment and of intelligence proper was possessed by such animals as dogs and apes. That was a quarter century ago. Unfortunately, there was such a complete absence of laboratory technique that no reliance can be placed upon his results. Those results, in contrast with those of most psychologists, indicated for Hobhouse the presence of practical judgment and the ability to learn through perception of results. The animal reasons from particulars to particulars without sensing the implied universal. A few animals achieve relatively simple "articulate ideas" but they do not reach truly abstract thought.

Apart from his *Mind in Evolution,* Hobhouse is best known in America for his *Morals in Evolution.* In much that he has written, but especially in this latter volume, in the latest edition, we find a clear statement of his position on social evolution. The history of various human institutions is sketched, the material being selected with consummate skill and organized with care. In the preceding pages much attention was devoted to this sketch as being an excellent introduction to Hobhouse. Here we find him at his best.

The phases of social evolution here sketched were law and justice, the position of women and marriage, inter-community relations, class and caste, and property and poverty. We shall not attempt to resummarize them here. In each aspect of the community's life Hobhouse found certain trends flowing toward a fairer and saner organization of man's group life.

There is one difficulty felt by all students of social evolution: since man lived countless centuries upon the earth before he invented permanent written records how is that early period to be studied? One fairly common answer has been to turn to the primitive societies of today. This Hobhouse did, making an exhaustive statistical analysis of a large number of ethnologists' reports upon primitive peoples in different parts of the world. The particular problem to which he addressed himself was the relation between social institutions and the methods of food-getting that obtained in the group. Broadly speaking he discovered that institutions improved and became more complex as food-getting techniques advanced.

The methodology of this study, as presented in *The Material Culture and Social Institutions of the Simpler Peoples,* has certain faults: the statistical unit is a vague and indefinite quantity; results may be complicated by diffusion, and such factors as varing densities of population not adequately taken into account. However, as a pioneering effort it blazes an important trail.

Of more fundamental importance is the work of this author in the field of social ethics. Here, in addition to its history in important phases, as just touched upon, he sets forth what it is conceived to be, on philosophical and psychological bases. He also indicates the relation of his code of ethics to present world problems.

On the psychological side, Hobhouse first sets forth his reasons for believing that rational and purposive conduct is possible to the individual. He does this in some detail because his whole system becomes meaningless without a world of rational self-directing individuals. The *will* rests upon feeling in the generic sense and it often happens that the distant end toward which the will directs conduct is not felt with sufficient power to overcome transient desires. Impulse-feeling is the raw material of human nature out of which is fashioned successively desire, volition, will.

Now the will may drive on toward ends that are rational and good (and it is argued that these come to the same thing in the end) or toward the irrational and bad. The irrational is the self-contradictory whether in individual or society. That individual is rational whose entire personality organization is consistent, and, as he necessarily lives in contact with other personalities, society must be consistent. Conflict must disappear from within the individual and his circle of friends and by inevitable extensions from the wider society, from the world, and ultimately from the universe. Only thus can we have a completely rational and good individual. Just as in the physical sciences we do not expect ultimately to find any exceptions to natural law, so in social ethics we need not expect to find factors refusing to fit into a scheme of the rational good. The basic word of that scheme is Harmony. We are to look forward to universal harmony. Every discord shall disappear from a symphony made up of the pipings of the obscurest shepherd and the noisiest bass drummer on earth and every conceivable type of noise maker in between. The very music of the spheres will underlie and give a tonal base to the whole structure of sound.

And yet how are we to be sure, in our hours of pessimism, that such is the case? How know that we do not rattle on aimlessly, purposelessly, and utterly without harmony? Our hope lies partly in the history of human society with its long-time trend toward a more harmonious world, partly in man's freedom of choice and collective self-direction so that with increasing knowlege we may expect increasing harmony, and partly in that reality is something besides matter and is in a measure directed by a spirit of harmony. Our hope is to be supported by three props; history, logic, and metaphysics.

One is tempted to try one's strength against these props. Already a bit of a mining operation has been attempted under the historic support but no hostile action will be directed against the logical or the metaphysical ones. To some minds they may seem impregnable; to others they fall of their own weight. And yet whatever one's opinion of a theory of the ultimate harmony of the universe, there can be little doubt that harmony as a working concept in human relations has value.

Hobhouse has indicated how his scheme of social harmony might be carried through in relation to every major problem confronting society today. Only a few of the more important have been reviewed to illustrate the approach and the method.

By way of clearing the ground he indicates that rights and duties are relative. The individual in a community has certain obligations, his *duties,* and certain claims upon the community, his *rights.* No rights, as such, are inviolable and yet rights are not to be thought of as entirely dependent upon the common welfare. Life must have the stability and security that comes with knowing what the rules of the game are in all ordinary circumstances.

A difficult point at which to apply this scheme of rights and duties is free contract. Abstractly one might suppose that the less constraint placed upon contracts between individuals or groups the better. However, since the strong may impose disastrous terms upon the weak, it is one of the obligations of the community to see that free contract does not contradict elementary justice. In the same way *rights* of nationality, *rights* of colonial powers to concessions in weaker countries, etc., are all relative to the total situation. Moreover, the whole structure of elementary rights stands or falls together. If a colonial power denies rights of nationality it will by inevitable extensions proceed to over-ride others until its power is based on naked force alone. Witness the British in South Africa and the Boer War. On that unhappy conflict, Hobhouse has expressed himself with the greatest vigor.

Rights vary with *needs,* and needs vary in urgency and in quantity. In either case the law of diminishing returns applies rigorously; a crust of bread means more to the hungry man than a banquet to one well fed. And as long as there are the hungry, society should tolerate no extravagent banquets. Any development of the few at the expense of the many runs contrary to the principle of harmony. Each person must share in the good of society in proportion to the capacity of his social personality.

Social justice requires that individual merit be found and rewarded—not an easy task. At the lowest, however, society should assure itself that every necessary worker received sufficient reward to maintain him in full civic efficiency. Differences in reward for the same kinds of work may be determined by quantity of output, and between different kinds of work by demand and supply. If society assures itself that no one is pushed below the civic minimum then a system of free exchange is justified.

Free exchange brings with it wealth for the more clever individual and with the wealth ordinarily comes larger freedom and greater power, Hobhouse holds that society should so regulate the use of wealth as to give the individual freedom but not power. And all wealth-holding should be conditional upon service to the community. Functionless wealth, growing largely out of inheritance, and ownership of natural resources, has no ethical defenses and should be destroyed. Since all wealth-holding is dependant upon the will of society it follows that the community shóuld establish safeguards to prevent the individual obtaining or using wealth in an anti-social way.

If production of wealth by the individual is to be replaced there are two important ways in which this may occur. There may be; (1) management by state or municipality, or (2) industrial self-government through coöperative guilds. The first has been fairly successful and might well be extended to include such commodities as milk and bread, though it is doubtful whether it could include all industry; the second must wait upon actual tests to determine its feasibility. Under the guild scheme all the workers in an industry, organized on a world basis, would decide the policy of the industry. A congress of guilds, with representatives of the public, would determine matters of relationship between guilds. One obvious problem of such an arrangement would lie in controlling the enormous power in the hands of a key industry like coal mining.

Whatever the method of production and distribution in society, an underlying problem, one most important and difficult of solution is how to develop an effective democracy. Majority rule is a make-shift and should be exercised with caution. It is tolerable only where the community is homogeneous in population. Every man's will should be taken into account, but how can this be? Democracy has difficulty not so much with a selfish common will as with getting any common will at all.

Real democracy requires as a synthetic principle the idea of community. All differences within the community are those of a family and are insignificant compared to the common interests. Ultimately there is only one community,—the human race. The natural tendency toward such a world community, foreshadowed by economic relations, by scientific associations, and in many other ways, is hindered by obsolete theories of the sovereign state. To hold that the supreme duty of the individual is to the political organization controlling a given geographic area is to fly in the face of obvious facts. Loyalties are tied to things so diverse as a group of blood relations and an international scientific society, and each set of loyalties renders complete loyalty to any of the others, including the state, impossible. The God-State of Hegel is absurd and if accepted blocks the path to a true international society. The sovereign state of today must become subordinate to a world organization of human society.

A few pages have been devoted in this volume to a discussion of sociology as a science. For Hobhouse the distinctive function of sociology is social morphology and its subject-mater the individual reacting in his normal human relationships. He would trace back the history of human institutions to early beginnings and ascertain both the line of development and the connection between one institution and another. By carrying out research along these lines we may in time be able to state certain social laws with complete assurance.

Now social laws are possible despite the fact that the individual has freedom of choice (that notion upon which Hobhouse insists so strongly) and that the world of humans we see about us seems far from predictable by any sort of law. For Hobhouse the law of probability makes individual freedom and social law compatible. If a large number of individuals must choose either A or B, and there are no factors more favorable to the choice of one than the other, then we may expect to find the same number preferring A as have chosen B. If a larger number chose A the reason lies in something other than freedom of choice and we may go about discovering that something. To the one who despairs of ever discovering social laws because of the topsy-turvy and entirely unpredictable world we live in, Hobhouse replies that social laws are like all scientific laws; they hold only when the required conditions are present. The simple formula for the law of gravity fits the case only when rigorously defined conditions are met. We may correctly speak of a law of demand and supply, and a law of diminishing returns, etc., and in time we may speak with equal confidence of many social laws now dimly visualized.

If we are ever able to formulate sociological laws much credit will be due to L. T. Hobhouse. During a long career he has turned his keenly analytical mind upon every phase of the social problem and while his limitations are obvious his high abilities become increasingly clear as one goes slowly through his works. Those works will long endure as the monument to a great intellect and a colossal attempt to bridge the distance between philosophy and a science of society.

BIBLIOGRAPHY

BOOKS BY HOBHOUSE

Democracy and Reaction. London, Unwin, 1904, vii + 244 pp. Republ. in pt. fr. the *Speaker.*

Development and Purpose, An Essay Toward a Philosophy of Evolution. Lond., Macmillan, 1913, xxix + 383 pp.

Elements of Social Justice. London, Allen & Unwin, 1922; N. Y., Henry Holt, 1922. viii + 247 pp.

The Labor Movement. Preface R. B. Haldane, 1st Ed. 1893; 2nd Ed. Lond., Unwin, 1898. vii + 98 pp.; 3rd Rev. Ed., N. Y., Macmillan, 1912, 159 pp.

Liberalism. N. Y., Holt, 1911, v + 254 pp. (Home Univ. Libr. of Mod. Knowl.)

Lord Hobhouse; a Memoir (Joint author—J. L. Hammond). Lond., Arnold, 1905, iv + 280 pp.

The Material Culture and Social Institutions of the Simpler Peoples, An Essay in Correlation. (Joint Author with G. C. Wheeler and M. Ginsberg) Lond., Chapman and Hall, 1915, iv + 299 pp.

The Metaphysical Theory of the State, A Criticism. Lond., Allen & Unwin, N. Y., Macmillan, 1918, 156 pp.

Mind in Evolution. (1st Ed.) Lond. & N. Y., Macmillan, 1901, xiv + 415 pp. (2nd Ed.) Lond., Macmillan, 1915, xix + 469 pp.

Morals in Evolution; A Study in Comparative Ethics, 1st Ed. Lond., Chapman & Hall, 1906 (2 Vols.) New Ed. Rev., N. Y., Holt, 1915, xvi + 648 pp.

Questions of War and Peace. Lond., Unwin, 1916, 233 pp.

The Rational Good; A Study in the Logic of Practice. London, Allen & Unwin, 1921; N. Y., Henry Holt, 1921. xxii + 237 pp.

Social Evolution and Political Theory. N. Y., Col. Univ. Press, 1911, ix + 218 pp.

Social Development, Its Nature and Conditions. Lond., Allen & Unwin, 1924, 348 pp.

Theory of Knowledge; A Contribution to Some Problems of Logic and Metaphysics. Lond., Methuen, 1896, xx + 627 pp.

World in Conflict. Lond., Unwin, 1915, 104 pp. "A series of articles contributed to the Manchester *Guardian* during March, April, and May 1915 and reprinted with additions." Note.

"Law and Justice," in *Representative Essays* by H. R. Steves & F. H. Ristine, 341-75.

IMPORTANT PERIODICAL WRITINGS

(Approximately in the order of their appearance)

"Ethical Basis of Collectivism," *Int. Jour. of Ethics* 8 :137-56.

"Laws of Hammurabi," *Liv. Age* 237 :250-3 Ap 25 '03.

"Question of the Lords," *Contemp.* 91 :1-11, Ja 1907.

"Constitutional Issue," *Contemp.* 91 : 312-8 Mr. '07.

"Editorial," *Sociological Rev.* 1 :1-11 '08.

"Prospects of Liberalism," *Contemp.* 93 : 349-58 Mr '08.

"Lords and the Constitution," *Contemp.* 96 : 641-51 D '09.

"Contending Forces," *English* R 4 : 359-71 Ja '10

"New Spirit in America," *Contemp.* 100 :1-10 Jl '11 same *Living Age* 270 :323-30 Ag5, '11.

"Prospects of Anglo-Saxon Democracy," *Atlan.* 109 :345-52 Mr '12.

"Review of Westermarck's Origin and Development of Moral Ideals," *Sociol.* R. 2 : p. 402 '09.

"Social Effects of War," *Atlantic* 115 :544-50 Ap '15.

"Soul of Civilization," *Contemp.* 108 :158-65 Ag '15.

REVIEWS OF WRITINGS OF HOBHOUSE

(The signs + and — before a review indicates the extent to which the reviewer regards the book favorably or unfavorably. The rating is from the Book Review Digest, not the author.)

Democracy and Reaction

+ — *Ann. Am. Acad.* 25 :603, My '05 (400 W). Ward W. Pierson.

+ + + *Int. J. Ethics.* G. P. Gooch 15 :499 Jl '05 (1890 W).

+ + + *J. Pol. Econ.* 14 :181 Mr '06 (1350 W).

J. Morley in his *Miscellanies.* 4 :267-326.

J. Morley in *19th Cent.* 57 :361.

+ + — *Nation* 80 :254 Mr. 30-'05 (1070 W).

+ *Outlook* 79 :502 F. 25 '05 (160 W).

+ + *Spectator* 94 :119 Ja 28 '05 (340).

+ + *Westminster Rev.* 163 :106 Ja.

Development and Purpose

A. L. A. Bkl. 10 :55 O '13.

Ath. 1913 1 :304 Mar. 15 (100 W).

+ — *Boston Transcript* My 14 '13 (580 W).

+ + — Hibbert, J. 12 :222 O '13 (2150 W).

Ind. (F. M. Stawell) 75 :570 S 4 '13 (700 W).

+ — *Int. Ethics* 24:94 O '13 (1700 W).
+ — *Nation* 97:163 Ag 21 '13 (1450 W).
+ — *Nature* 82:3 S 4 '13 (300 W).
+ N. Y. *Times* 18:396 Jl 13 '13 (800 W).
   N. Y. *Times* 18:676 N. 30 '13 (280 W).
+ *Outlook* 104:825 Ag 9 '13 (250 W).
+ *Spec* 110:849 My 17 '13 (130 W).

Elements of Social Justice
   Nation and Ath. 31:227 My 13 '22 (1000 W).
+ *Sat. R.* 133:122 F 4 '22 (400 W).
   Survey 48:628 Ag 15 'aa (150 W).
   The Times (London) *Lit. Sup.* p. 847 D. 15 '21
     (50 W).
+ *The Times* (London) *Lit. Sup.* p. 2, Ja 5 '22
     (1100 W).
   Wis Lib. Bul. 18: 213 O '22.

Lord Hobhouse: A Memoir
   Am. Hist. R. (Geo. M. Wrong). 12:141 O '16.
     (770 W).
+ *Ath.* 1905 2:858 D 23 (960 W).
+ Lond. *Times* 5:6 Ja 5 '06 (840 W).
+ *Nation* 82:327 Ap. 19 '06 (1650 W).
+ — *Sat. R.* 101:210 F. 17 '06 (220 W).
+ *Spec.* 96:386 Mr 10 '06 (240 W).

The Labour Movement
   Outlook (Eng.) 2:86 Aug. 20 '98.

Liberalism
   A. L. A. Bkl. 8:149 D '11.
+ — *Spec.* 107:248 Ag. 12 '11 (1800 W).

Material Culture and Social Institutions of the Simpler Peoples
+ *Int. J. Ethics* 26:144 O '15 (150 W).
+ *Nature* 95:672 Ag 19 '15 (200 W).
+ *Spec.* 115:185 Ag. 7 '15 (230 W).

Metaphysical Theory of the State
+ — *Am. Pol. Sci. R.* 13:318 My '19 (700 W).
+ — *Hibbert, J.* 17:328 Ja '19 (1900 W).
   Sat. R. 126:1164 D. 14 '18 (70 W).
+ *Spec.* 121:551 N. 16 '18 (700 W).

+ Springf'd *Republican* p. 6 Je 16 '19 (600 W).
+ — *The Times* (London) Lib. Sup. p. 53211 7 '18 (800 W).

Mind in Evolution

Ath. 1902 1:266-7 Mr. 1.
Nation. 75:313 O. 16 '02.
C. L. Morgan in *Mind* 28:103.

Morals in Evolution (Revised Edition)

A. L. A. Bkl. 12:99 N. '15.
+ *Ann. Am. Acad.* 63:295 Ja '16 (60 W).
+ *Int. J. Ethics* 26:298 Ja '16 (950 W).
+ *Lit. D.* 51:1091 N. 13 '15 (350 W).
+ *Nature* 96:83 S 23 '15 (870 W).
N. Y. *Times* 21:13 Ja 9 '16 (60 W).
+ + — *Philos. R.* 16:527 S. '07 (6000 W).
+ Springfield *Repub.* p. 5 S 23 '15 (1200 W).

Morals in Ev. (1st Edition).

+ + — *Ann. Am. Acad.* (Carl Kelsey) 30:180 Jl '07 (710 W).
+ + — *Ath.* 1907 1:784 Je 29 (250 W).
+ + — *Hibbert J.* (H. Rashdall) 5:921 Jl '07 (4140 W).
+ + — *Hibbert J.* (G. E. Underhill) 5:928 Jl '07 (2410 W).
+ + *J. Philos.* (Norman Wilde) 183 Mr. 28 '07 (1930 W).
+ London *Times* 5:414 D. 14 '06 (1750 W).
+ + *Nation* 84:568 Je 20 '07 (940 W).
+ + N. Y. *Times* 12:93 F 16 '07 (1590 W).
+ + *Outlook* 85:523 Mr. 2 '07 (330 W).
+ *Sat. R.* 103:400 Mr 30 '07 (1150 W).

Questions of War and Peace

+ *Nation* 104:48 Ja 11 '17 (300 W).
Nation 105:297 S 13 '17 (450 W).
N. Y. *Br Lib News* 3:187 D '16.
+ *Spec.* 118:19 Ja 6 '17 (1350 W).
The *Times* (London) *Lit. Sup.* p. 311 Je 29 '16 (190 W).

Rational Good

Booklist 18:105 Ja. '22.
+ *New Republic* 28:353 N. 16 '21 (1400 W).

+ *Spec.* 127:213 Ag. 13 '21 (230 W).
Springfield *Republican* P. 8 Je 11 '21 (240 W).

Social Development; Its Nature and Conditions
 Am. J. Soc. (A. W. Small) (30:216 S. '24 (1950 W).
 Boston *Transcript.* p. r My 24 '24 (520 W).
 Cleveland p. 93 D '24.
+ — *Nation and Ath.* (C. E. Ayres) 34:932 Mr 29 '24 (150 W).
 New Repub. 39:164 J. 2 '24 (1100 W).
+ — *New Statesman* 22:764 Ap. 5 '24 (950 W).
 N. Y. Tribune p. 25 Jl. 27 '24 (60 W).
 Outlook 137:112 My 21 '24 (10 W).
+ — *Sat. Rev.* 137:88 Ja 26 '24 (650 W).
+ *Survey* 52:244 My 15 '24 (950 W).
— + *Times* (Lond.) *Lit. Sup.* p. 260 My 1 '24 (1200 W).

Social Evolution and Political Theory
+ — *Am. J. Soc.* (A. W. Small) 17:546 Ja. '12 (900 W).
 A. L. A. Bkl. 8:302 Mr. '12.
 Am. Pol. Sci. R.; (T. D. Eliot) 6:608, N '12 (300 W).
 Ann. Am. Acad. (T. D. Eliot) 43:339 S. '12 (500 W).
+ *Ath.* 1912 1:308 Mr. 16 (400 W).
+ *Dial* 52:287 Ap. 1, '12 (280 W).
+ *Educ. R.* 43:536 My '12 (10 W).
+ — *J. Pol. Econ.* 20:970 N. '12 (470 W).
+ *Nation* 95:63 Jl. 18 '12 (180 W).
 Sociological R. 5:169 '12 (G. P. Gooch).

Theory of Knowledge
 Dial 23:215-7 O. 17 (F. C. Sharp).
 Ind. 48:1335 O. 1.
 Philos. R. (J. E. Creighton) 7:77-82 Ja. '98.

ARTICLES ON HOBHOUSE

"Leonard T. Hobhouse and the Neo-liberal Theory of the State," H. E. Barnes in *Am. J. Sociol.* 27:442-85 Ja. '22.
"English and American Philosophy Since 1800," A. K. Rogers, pp. 348-351.
"Critical Miscellanies," John Morley, v. 4 pp. 265-326.